AS A CENTER OF CONSCIOUSNESS

YOU ARE
INVISIBLE

By

RAYMOND CHARLES BARKER

INCLUDING THE NEVER-BEFORE-IN-PRINT
IMMEASURABLE MIND

DeVorss Publications
Marina del Rey, California

ISBN: 0-87516-576-1
Library of Congress Catalog Number: 73-1654

DeVorss & Company, Publisher
P.O. Box 550
Marina del Rey, CA 90294

Printed in The United States of America

YOU ARE INVISIBLE

CONTENTS

A WORD FROM THE AUTHOR

Someone going through some old files at the New York church* where I served as Founder-Minister for thirty-three years found a manuscript of a lecture I gave at the church some twenty years ago.

I had no memory of its existence, but after reading it I became so enthusiastic about it that I knew it had to be published. I shared it with the editors at DeVorss & Company, publishers of this new paperback edition of my book *You Are Invisible*. They shared my enthusiasm and requested that it appear in the new edition. I have called it *Immeasurable Mind*.

Immeasurable Mind has never before appeared in print. You will find it a mind-stretching article, which it is meant to be. It may take a few readings to really lift your consciousness to fresh vistas of what you really are and where you really are.

After many printings in hardcover, I welcome back *You Are Invisible*, with fresh and vital material added to it in this new paperback edition.

May 1986

---

* The First Church of Religious Science, New York City.

YOU ARE INVISIBLE

CHAPTER

I

THE LEAVES
MUST FALL

—

Your most priceless possession is your mind, and what you are doing with it *at this instant* is significant, not what you did with it yesterday or a number of years ago. Mind is invisible, but its *now* activity is visible to all who know you.

The only form of life that hangs onto the past is man. When nature has brought in colder weather in the autumn, the leaves fall. They fall because the tree has finished its annual cycle and it needs them no more. The tree has no fear as it lets go of each leaf. It has no regret at letting go of something that has served its purpose. Those leaves will never return, but there will be new leaves in the spring to serve a new purpose.

We cannot endow the tree with memory of past winters and past springs, because memory is an emotional experience. We are the only form of life that has memory, as we know it. Lesser forms of animals can be taught to run through a maze or perform other feats which they have learned through trial and error, usually supplemented by a reward. The animal world operates to a great extent by instinct. Instinctively certain creatures hoard food for the winter, and instinctively they stop hoarding when spring arrives and food is plentiful.

Man, often involuntarily, hangs onto the past. He hoards old memories in his subconscious mind, where they may lie dormant for a long time, and if they are negative they may suddenly pop up to trouble him. Memories of pleasant or worthwhile experiences are never harmful. Those of you who have undergone psychotherapy or psychoanalysis know how astounded you were at some of the old thought patterns and beliefs that were unearthed in the process. Many of them were frightening and you did not want to face the fact that you have been storing up destructive motivations in your subconscious for years. Perhaps you have been hoarding a great many negatives since early childhood.

This does not apply only to people who have distressed minds. It applies to everyone. Those of us who are quite well adjusted to life, and able to function quite normally, have reserved some storage space in the subconscious for old memories, and often, when we least expect it, one of these phantoms from the past comes to light.

I frequently do a considerable amount of reading at night. Occasionally I pause and look out of the window. What happens during that moment of relaxed attention? Quite often some long-buried negative pops through the trapdoor of my mind. It may be a problem that I haven't thought of for years, or it may be a fairly recent hurt or resentment. It arrives at my conscious level of mind with power and authority. It wants me to do a repeat performance. Something that hurt my feelings wants me to be saddened all over again. Someone I didn't like wants me to hate all over again.

It is quite possible for me to take fifteen minutes and review the whole episode, get myself all worked up, and become emotionally involved once more with something that, once forgotten, should stay forgotten.

I am well aware, and you should be too, that old hurts and old rejections arrive at the threshold of consciousness in order to get out. If you take your hands off—by that I mean stop reviewing and rehearsing the past event—you can help that negative get out of your subconscious mind. Say something like this: *Get out of my life. You have come this far. Go out into the nothingness where you belong. You have finished your act. I want you no more.*

In order to do this you must have the willingness to let go of the past. Let the leaves fall. I do not mean get rid of everything you own. I am talking of consciousness and the operation of ideas in mind. The motivation of mind is to proceed.

A good statement to make here is: *I freely let go of the past. I freely let go of that which yet will be. I am a now person in a now experience.*

FACE THE NOW

There are changes in the thinking of psychologists, psychiatrists, and psychoanalysts, just as there are changes in the experimental techniques of nuclear scientists, in the modes of operation of city planners, and in the concepts of those who are leaders in industry, education, the general field of health, and so on.

Ever since the time of Freud, it has been the popular assumption of a great many experts in the field of psychology and phychiatry that by the time you are six years old every basic pattern of life is already formed in your subconscious mind. Each pattern takes over and you follow through on it. This is why many of today's psychiatrists and psychoanalysts who believe in plumbing the depths of the "unconscious" discover that the problem of a fifty-year-old person started in his early childhood.

I believe William James, professor of psychology at Harvard University around the turn of the century, gave us a little longer time to form those patterns. He placed the age when they were firmly set at twenty-one.

I am not a psychiatrist or a psychologist, but I believe that any pattern can be changed at any time, if you so desire. Mind is not inflexible. Mind is creative. Mind is always trying to go forward. It is not trying to go back.

That is why I was pleased several years ago when a forward-looking psychiatrist, Dr. William Glasser, wrote a book entitled *Reality Therapy*. In it he expressed his viewpoint that it is not necessary to probe the past, but it is imperative to help the patient relate to the now. He emphasizes the need for every mentally disturbed individual, young or mature, to learn responsibility in the now. He stresses the need for every individual who requires psychiatric help to be closely involved with at least one other person, but preferably with several; the need to love and be loved, and the need to feel that he or she is worthwhile.

These are tenets with which we of the New Thought

Movement agree: the need for individual responsibility, the need for communication with others, the need to love and be loved, and the need for self-expression, which can be interpreted as worthwhileness. We believe that all of these experiences should take place in the now, and that in reality there is only the split-second of current awareness. There has been a past, and there will be a future, but at this instant, as a thinking, feeling, expressing consciousness, there is only this moment in your life.

A current television commercial begins, "Today is the first day of the rest of your life." That's not a bad concept when we remember that your today is tomorrow, and that your this year is your next year. You are creating your future right now, and it is not dependent upon what happened in your past.

CLEAR OUT THE OLD

When you say, "I can't remember what is wrong," perhaps that means that you are aware of what is right. Sometimes we need to forget as well as remember. But when we forget, let us do it thoroughly by clearing consciousness of the old, unwanted idea.

I believe, among other things, that one of the purposes of prayer is to teach us to forget. I think that no matter what method you use, whether it be old or new, whether it be of one vocabulary or another, one purpose of it—even the most affirmative spiritual treatment—has been to negate something that we no longer want in consciousness.

We have had too many years of taking in new ideas without clearing out the old ones. Therefore, in many instances, the new ideas have merely put a new coat of paint on the same old building. It has made it look new, and seem new, but it isn't new at all.

I know people who have studied the New Thought teaching for years, yet, while they don't know it, they are still basically Presbyterians, Baptists, Methodists, Episcopalians or whatever they were before they came to us. They are still indoctrinated with the old ideas, and may I say rightly so, because they have not learned to forget. They have just taken in an inflow of new ideas, and new ideas alone won't do it. They are always transformed through old mechanisms. It doesn't make any difference whether the ideas are political, scientific, economic, religious, or what.

It is very difficult to take a new idea and use it as a new idea when it is accepted by, employed by, and operated through the ideas that have been there before. This is why, several years ago, I made a change in the format of our Sunday-morning service. I deliberately withdrew hymns and solos because I believe that to present a new idea you have to present it in a new way. I withdrew the setting, the atmosphere which would inevitably adulterate the new with the old. There have been few complaints.

MEMORY VERSUS "FORGETTERY"

Years ago there were two famous New Thought lecturers in this country, William Walker Atkinson and David Bush. They were competitors, though they both spoke of uses of the mind. Atkinson gave a series of one-week's free lectures and then had a five-night closed class on

"How to Develop a Perfect Memory." He charged a fee for this. Atkinson went to all of the major cities, where he hired a hall similar to our Carnegie Hall in New York City. He always filled it and at the end of the series everyone had "the key to perfect memory." David Bush, aware of his competitor's tactics, followed, about a month later, into each of the cities Atkinson had covered. He would hire the same hall, do the same advertising, give his free classes for a week, and then his paid classes the second week. However, he talked on "How to Develop a Perfect Forgettery."

These two men covered all the major cities in the United States for several years and were prosperous. Like all pioneers they had hit upon a truth, but they should have reversed the circuit. David Bush should have gone in first with "Forgettery," to be followed a month later by William Atkinson with his "Memory." They had the cart before the horse, because by the time all of the people had learned to develop perfect memories, their minds were so cluttered with past experiences and past ideas that they had a hard time learning to forget.

You and I have found this to be true in our work with Mind. It is particularly hard to forget negatives of the past, because we don't forget anything that hits us with an emotional impact. We may think we have forgotten, but it lies buried until it is released.

I am reminded here of a dream I had a few years ago. Its content portrayed a battle that must have been dormant in my subconscious for a long, long time. Some years earlier I had a definite dispute with a man who was condemning me, unjustly I thought. I got him off my pathway. A couple of years later he went on to the next plane of life. I thought little of it and didn't mourn him, because I am not a hypocrite. When he had been gone for ten or twelve years, I had a very unpleasant dream of fighting him physically. He was knocking me around and I was knocking him. When I awoke, right after the dream, I said, "Okay. So he is still in my subconscious mind with that amount of power."

Immediately I got up, left my bedroom, went to the desk, put on the light, and sat down. "All right, John," I said. "The image of you in my subconscious mind is not going to do this again. I have finished this fight. Wherever you are on your pathway, I release you. I bless you." Then I said: "Subconscious mind, I want this memory pattern stopped. I don't want to carry it around any more." I didn't know it was down there. I hadn't thought of him for years. But the whole thing came up in the dream world, which is another trapdoor through which the subconscious can appear.

There was a distinct feeling of anger in this dream, and I went to work on my spiritual treatment. I went to work on my pattern, not his. He is all right, wherever he is. I worked for a good ten minutes on my subconscious mind. I have not had the dream since, and I probably never will, because I cleared my mind of that violent negative as soon as it exposed itself to me.

EMOTIONAL IMPACT

It is extremely difficult to forget anything that hits us with an emotional impact. We can forget the trivial, we can forget the casual, but we do not easily forget things that are delivered into our minds under heavy emotion. Emotion is the key to Life. Emotion is the law of living. This is why the ancient teaching that the primary aspect of God is Love may be more important than the aspect of a Divine Mind with any other quality.

It is well established psychologically that the only thing that really affects us is emotion; we are emotional people, and emotion is the creative power of the mind. This is why balanced religion has always taught the power of love. One of the reasons why the teaching of Jesus caught on so quickly in the Roman Empire was that he was a symbol of love. He was not a symbol of war or of hate. Being the symbol of love, he interested people much more than did their old gods of hate and of war.

Emotions are the cornerstone of life. Yesterday carries into today only through our emotions, because the memory field is a field of emotional memory. This is why you cannot remember a casual incident that happened ten years ago, but you can remember a heartbreak or some equivalent unpleasantness that shook you up emotionally at that time. The remembrance of the evils of the past is a part of the nature of the mind until the mind is cleared through spiritual treatment. Nature arranged this because nature expects its creation to clear its own thought.

Man is the creation of God as Mind. You and I have not sought to clear our minds at all times. We have wanted someone else to do it for us. Down through the ages, men and women have devised many ways, many paths, many prayer books, many prayer wheels, many statues, many novenas, many saviors, because they wanted someone else to clear their thought, when, of course, this cannot be done. We have to clear our own thought.

You stand isolated like an island. You are you. You are not the savior, the prophet, or the saint. You are you. I am that which I am, and I never can be less. Therefore, if I am that which I am, then no man can clear my thought but myself. No one can change my belief but my own mind. No one can get rid of the past save by deliberately saying to the past, "Be gone. Thou art no longer a part of me." I have to say to that which emotionally crippled me ten years ago, twenty years ago, or three days ago, "Get thee behind me, Satan: thou art an offense unto me."

Emotion binds, emotion retains, emotion holds. What you do not want to remember is held in memory by emotion and not by common sense. You can say to it: *I no longer give you, the idea, any more emotional support. I declare that you have operated in me long enough. You have managed me long enough. I now declare that you convert yourself into a positive, healthy emotion.*

This is turning fear into faith, rejection into acceptance, disease into health, and hate into love. This can be done.

TAKE THE HURT OUT OF LIFE

You take the hurt out of life by first admitting you have it. You get some understanding of why you have it, and finally you say: "I will now withdraw my need for it. I no longer need to justify the present by the past. I no longer need to justify my present inadequacies merely on the basis of something that happened years or even weeks ago. I am emotionally interested in the new concept of what I am, and I refuse to remember what I was. I am intrigued by what I can become, and I no longer need to remember the hurts that made me what I was."

This is tremendously important. Most people do not like what they are. Therefore they revert to the past rather than accept the present. When you accept yourself as Life living this day, as Mind thinking this day, and as Love loving this day, you do not need to go to the past.

Jesus said, "No man, having put his hand to the plow, and turning back, is fit for the kingdom of God." A plow moves forward. The person behind the plow has to know where he is going. He has to know where to turn around to come back. He is so busy knowing what is to be done that he does not need to look behind him to see the furrow that is finished.

Life is the progressive action of the now, becoming the future. In order to move from here to there, I have to take up the anchors that I put down to keep me where I have been. Many people feel that it is very comfortable to be anchored somewhere. The anchor drags in the past. It deters them. They find that they are not moving forward. Yet they do nothing about it until Wisdom comes to the fore. Then they pull up the anchors—the negatives that are holding them down—and they are able to go full steam ahead. Having made the start, it is possible to become so fascinated with the course ahead that you can completely forget about the point from which you have come.

When this happens, you can say to the hurts of yesterday, "I can't remember you, except as an incident." You can say to the future, "I grasp you. I want to go in a creative, progressive action forward, impelled by a Mind that is God, and a Life that is lived, a Love that is great, and a Power that responds to the good."

Accept the memories of the great experiences which brought you joy. They need not be erased, because they are valuable, and the emotions that created them will hold them fast. It is only the negative, destructive memories that need to go, and you now know how to get rid of them.

GIVE THE PAST NO POWER

The past holds power as long as you feel that the past is greater than the present. As long as you nourish the past so as not to have to compete with the present, the past has you enthralled. The way to be rid of the past is to see it as experience and growth and nothing else. But we are so enmeshed in the personalities of the past, the situations of the past, that we slip from the present into the past and we become past people working in the present.

There are two very interesting, simple sentences of Scripture, written by the first Isaiah, who wrote the first third of the Book of Isaiah, at a time when the people were in captivity in Babylon. It was a time of great spiritual progress, even though they were very unhappy living, not as slaves, but as a foreign minority in a distant country, and they wanted to go home.

Like most of us, these people talked about the past, the good old days, and they kept saying to themselves, "Oh, if only things could be the way they were." They lamented, they wept, and the older generation kept on saying, "Oh, if only we could have things as they were." It is then that Isaiah speaks up, saying, "Remember ye not the former things, neither consider the things of old. Behold, I will do a new thing; now it shall spring forth; shall ye not know it?"

His meaning is clear. If your attention is so fixed upon the old patterns, the old habits, the things that used to be, the people that used to be, then you will not even see the new that I make. "Remember ye not former things," Isaiah said, "neither consider the things of old." Why? Because "I will do a new thing; now it shall spring forth; shall ye not know it?"

What Isaiah said hundreds of years ago applies equally well to us today. You and I are the people of that which shall be. We are not the people of that which has been.

One of the great advantages of being a part of the New Thought Movement is that we are not a part of that which has been. We are a part of that which is. It is good that we cannot trace our religious lineage back more than a hundred years. It is constructive that we cannot go back and claim that we are New Thought people because of what we were; we are New Thought people because of what we are. That sounds like a paradox, but it is a truth. It is a truth, and we have proven it.

CHAPTER

II

YOUR SUCCESS
MECHANISM

You are energy in action. Energy is invisible and only the results of its performance can be seen. Similarly, it is only what you produce that people can see.

In the entire universe there is a Divine rhythm. There is an ebb and flow. Everything is action. Everything is movement. There is nothing static anywhere. If you were a physicist you could look at the sink in your laboratory or at a piece of physical apparatus and know exactly what tremendous action was taking place in either of them. You wouldn't be able to see it, but you would know that this action is there, because you would be familiar—as many of us are—with the atomic theory that every object, animate or inanimate, is made up of countless numbers of invisible particles known as atoms. In each atom a certain number of electrons are revolving around a nucleus in a precise pattern that never varies. Such precise patterns of movement occur in the vast planetary systems of the cosmos.

The scientist calls this perfect movement "energy in action."

This invisible and orderly action takes place in your favorite armchair, in the mattress you sleep on and in every item in your home. It takes place in your body and in mine, and it takes place everywhere in the universe. It is a basic principle devised by Creative Intelligence and disclosed to the intellect of man through prolonged research.

Everything is motion, everything is energy, and everything is in flow. When you think of this, you realize what a vitality there is to existence.

We are the movement of the spirit, we are the action of life, and we are that pulsating, rhythmic consciousness in which Infinite Motivation is taking place. Individually each one of us is energy in action and we are able consciously to direct this energy in our own lives if we are willing to work for understanding and to make the effort to put this understanding to use.

YOU ARE SUCCESS-ORIENTED

Inbuilt into your consciousness there is a success mechanism. I don't know when this took place in evolutionary time, but at any rate you have it, because you are it. You are Mind individualized. That's what you really are. We have already said that we exist in a universe of energy, and we know that our physical bodies are composed of energy, but very few people think of their minds as energy, or realize that the process of consciousness is a movement of energy under specific direction which the individual gives it. Energy is creative power, and your thought is energy. Therefore, every thought you think causes something to happen. Casual thinking, while not very effective, is recorded and stored in your subconscious mind for some later use. But when you think with a purpose, and let your emotions take a part in the process, something definite will result.

In other words, you make a decision with the conscious mind and you carry it out with the subconscious mind. This is the process which I have called your "success mechanism." You are free to use it as you will.

YOUR SUBCONSCIOUS POWER

What you are in your experience is what you are subconsciously, not consciously. It was Sigmund Freud who discovered that you are what your subconscious mind is. This is what we believe today, and in order to adjust our concepts so that the newcomer to our way of thinking is at ease, we call the subconscious mind the soul. We call it this because it is undoubtedly what the mystics and the great teachers have been talking about in their writings.

Some would-be doubter once told me that he couldn't find the word subconscious in the entire Bible. Of course he couldn't, because it isn't there. The word wasn't invented until in the 1800's. Every generation develops a new vocabulary, and we are using current vocabulary in order to explain what we are talking about. The subconscious mind, which is the creative mind of the individual, is the beginning and the end of all experience. In saying this I do not sidestep the conscious mind.

In our definition we call it the spirit. The conscious mind is the spirit and the subconscious mind is the soul, and the interaction of the two results in what we call body, or form, or experience. You can control this interaction and have the experiences, the successes, the joys of life that you choose.

YOU ARE LARGELY SUBCONSCIOUS

Very little conscious thought actually takes place in your life, or in mine, in an average day. The great bulk of your activities from the time you arise until the time you go to sleep will be entirely subconscious, or, we might say, automatic. This includes getting up, how you awaken, how you dress, the kind of food you eat all day, the means you use to get to your office and back—or to whatever place you are going. It includes the way you spend your evening and your preparation for going to bed.

If you are in the business world, the financial world, or in any of the professions you undoubtedly will have decisions to make during the day. In that case you do use conscious thought as a means of setting your subconscious to work on a certain idea. But the bulk of everyone's existence is subconscious, and this is right. This is the way life operates.

Under the circumstances—knowing that the subconscious mind does the work—you can see the importance of giving the right motivations to it. That's what we do with the success mechanism when we are using it to produce success. We implant into the subconscious—usually audibly—the ideas we want to materialize. We do this firmly, and often with considerable repetition, and then we let the creative power of the subconscious go to work and bring about the realization of whatever it is we desire.

When we express the concept that all men are born equal, we refer to the fact that they all are born with a success mechanism. Various cultural patterns, environmental patterns, or family patterns may prevent this success mechanism from operating, but that does not mean that it isn't there. It is in every person, and regardless of individual situations, it can be known, can be activated, and can be experienced. All of this takes conscious effort, based on a conscious decision to direct the action of the subconscious.

STEPS YOU CAN TAKE

Many of you will ask the question, "If I have a success mechanism, why do I fail in so many areas of my life?" There are as many answers as there are problems. But the first thing is that we are just awakening to the fact that we have this success mechanism. People have been using it since the beginning of history but the average person has never been told that he had it. We have expected kings and emperors, presidents and scientists to have it, but we didn't know we had it.

Here in America, after the Industrial Revolution, we expected every millionaire to have it, but those who were not millionaires were not expected to have it. Then research and a vast amount of experience disclosed that you and I and all other individuals do have this success mechanism inbuilt from the beginning of time. Whether you use it or not is another question. Whether you decide to go on the side of greatness or not is your own personal affair.

First of all, remember that you are a success mechanism. Second, you are energy in action. You are a producer. Things happen because of you. You can only awaken motivation in the subconscious mind by conscious thought.

You will find it helpful if you say audibly: "I am a success mechanism and I have decided to use this equipment in the way it was intended to be used, because every individual is a unit of production. I am a unit of production."

Then watch your negatives. Here is an illustration.

Do you remember the last time you were depressed? In your depression, temporary or latent, you reactivated every unpleasant thing that had happened in your life. You went back and reviewed the list. You reactivated every item on the list and this increased your depression. Many times you wept. But fortunately, the depression didn't last forever. It finally went on its way.

If you would take the same amount of time, the same amount of mental energy, to reactivate every pleasant thing that has ever happened to you, you would get astonishing results. Every pleasant thing that has ever happened to you is still an active pattern in your subconscious mind and it can be reactivated. It can be pondered. It can be mulled over. It can be considered. When you start working this way on the pleasantness of the present and the pleasantness of the past, you begin to get new ideas, new impulsions, and new intuitive flashes. You begin to get what the world would call inspiration, and you begin

to look out at the world and see it in a positive, challeng-
ing light.

SET YOURSELF FREE

It has been my decision that I will not live in a world of
strain and struggle, because I don't have to. But I had to
set myself free. It says in the Bible that *the Truth sets you
free.* It is the truth of your own self that sets you free.

If you live in a world of struggle and strain, perhaps it
is because you enjoy being overbusy, overtired, and com-
plaining. Maybe you seek out little frustrations so you
can talk about them to your friends and relatives. Maybe
you take world problems on your own shoulders, which
you have no cause to do.

You and I exist in something that is not only Infinite;
it is indestructible and eternal. So we are still only at the
beginning level of our thought evolution, but I believe
we can speed up the process by knowing that it is self-
search, and not a search of the universe, that sets us on
the right track. This goes right back to the ancient dictum
know thyself.

For a long time in our self-development we didn't want
to know ourselves, because we had been told that what we
were wasn't healthy, or good, or right. In other words, according to the old line of thinking, we were sinners. Now
we've changed that. We are willing to look at ourselves
and see something valuable and creative, and this, despite
all of our mistakes, is the most important factor in our
experience.

"BE STILL AND KNOW THAT I AM GOD"

To many who are not familiar with our thinking, this statement, applied to an individual, is considered blasphemous. But as we interpret it, there is a Divine creative center in each and every one of us. When we say, "Be still and know that I *am* God," we mean that I am the potential, I am the creativity, I am the possibility, I am that which shall be. I am not that which was.

People of wisdom measure themselves in terms of today and the future. But average persons measure themselves in terms of the past. Ask them to describe their lives and they describe life entirely in terms of the past. Go to a creative mind and say: "Tell me about your life." He or she describes what they are doing right now, not what they did years ago. They talk about what they are doing now and what they are expecting to do. That's creativity. That's a *now* person in a *now* experience, creating something greater in the period to come. That is a person who knows he has a success mechanism and is using it.

Such a person has accepted himself as he is, not as he was. You are what you are, and that is good. You can direct it. You can become more of it. You can experience its benefits. That's what we are trying to do. We are trying definitely, with *intent* and *purpose*, to have health, to have ease, to have order, to have peace within ourselves, to have self-expression, and to have loving relationships with others. We can have all of these because all of the equipment necessary is already within us.

We do not plead to a deity for what we want. We are it. We do not beseech the gates of heaven, because your next thought is the gate of heaven. We are not seeking to change anyone else. We are seeking to determine our individual selves: What we are, what we are going to be, what we are going to do, and what we are going to become.

SELF-DETERMINATION

Even though we read of disaster and violence in our newspapers each day, and hear of conflicts and injustices on radio and television, the universe is still a spiritual system. It is a beneficent system and when you and I know how to live intelligently in it, we will get intelligent results from it. I have always been interested in noting that one of the last places most people apply their intelligence is to their own way of living. We will use our innate intelligence in our business. We do that because we have to make money. We use it in our homes in order to be comfortable. We occasionally use it in family and social relationships because it makes for peace and order rather than discord and a good family fight.

Why not decide today to use your intelligence on yourself, about yourself, because this innate intelligence is Life itself? It operates whether you use it or not, whether you direct it or not. It is not something you induce. It is something that is already taking place. Life is. Creativity is. The action of Life is taking place.

If there is anything in the world that mankind has not wanted, and has sought out every means possible to prevent, it is self-determination. This has been one of the great holds of organized religion, because such religion tells you what to do. You don't have to think to do it yourself. People have manufactured their gods in order to have someone outside of themselves tell them what to do. But the individual can grow only when he determines his own experience.

The day usually comes when you take your life into your own hands and decide what you are going to do with it. For some people, however, that day never comes. They go through their entire lifetime bounced about by what they feel are the winds of chance. They are tossed around by what the world believes, what the group in which they are functioning believes, and what the culture in which they are functioning is creating. These individuals go from birth to death and many of them live happily; many of them live well; but they are missing the whole reason for being here. I am sure the whole reason for being here is self-discovery, self-determination, and self-programming.

You and I know that this is true. Whether we practice it or not is another question. We know that we are self-determining agents in a universe that responds to us as we respond to it. Therefore, you and I are doing one thing and one thing only. We are directing consciousness. We are not manipulating events. We are changing, or directing, or determining what on the inside will produce what we want on the outside.

But most people have wanted external disciplines and not internal investigations. They want to be told what to do. I'm sure that the power of external authority is necessary in external affairs. But when it comes to self-investigation, when it comes to finding out what I am or what you are, we move into a whole new field of thinking, feeling, and experimentation. We move into the field of self-exploration.

SELF-EXPLORATION

I have already used the Biblical quotation "Be still and know that I am God." Most people have interpreted this to mean that we should be quiet in church because in some way God is there. Of course Creative Intelligence is no more in church than It is in Disneyland or in your favorite motion-picture theater. Whatever It is, It is everywhere. But man, generally speaking, has not wanted to be still—to still his intellect long enough to realize that whatever the Nature of Life is, he is it. He has to be it right here and right now or he never will be it.

Of course we have had the carrot out in front of the donkey all of these ages, believing that someday the good, the great, and the wonderful would take place. That someday, usually after death, the individual would reach a state of perfection. We know now that this isn't so. You take the whole self with you wherever you are going and no one improves by dying. Therefore, we are interested in doing whatsoever we desire right here and right now. Be still and know that what you are right now is the essence of life, the nature of the universe. It is the creative power. It is the whole thing.

Don't dodge this because you don't want to accept the responsibility. Stop blaming the world. Stop blaming your fellow men. Begin to examine yourself. If you are all the power that is, then you are all intelligence and you are all action. You are all love. You are all possibility. If you are all of this you can do with it as you select, because you have free will.

When you are willing to take the responsibility that goes with free will, then you have it. Otherwise the world runs you. Otherwise you are run by the opinions, the beliefs of some group, whether it be a social group, a family group, or a political group.

When you function in these groups, but function as an individual, you are free. You function wherever you are with your own definite "explored opinion." How many of your present opinions about the world are explored opinions or just assumed opinions? There is a great difference between assuming an opinion, a belief, or assuming a conviction and exploring it before accepting it.

In this connection, Mrs. Eddy, founder of the Christian Science Movement, made a statement about standing porter at the gate of thought, meaning that you should be the guardian, having discretion about what is admitted to your mind. Take some time to sort out and to remember that anything that has been ingested does not have to be digested.

When we say that the individual is God, is that the only Divine Intelligence there is? Of course not. You individualize that which, while it can be individualized, can never be fully individualized. There is always the All of which we individualize a part. There is that which runs the cosmos. There is that which operates the farthest star. There is that which is the Eternal Causation of ideas; that which is always taking place, always expressing Itself.

But that doesn't minimize what you are. We've made man and woman seem mean, small, and unimportant. I'm talking about the older philosophies, when I say that. They have always minimized the greatness of the individual. They have seen all the mistakes of the individual, and we see them today. Far too often, our attention has been riveted on what's wrong with the individual, not what's right.

You are not your mistakes. You are a success mechanism. Learn not to make mistakes seem important. You, as a wiser, self-aware, creative individual, will be a tremendous gift to society. But you as the mean, the little, the cluttered, the hampered, the worried, the fearful—you can't make any contribution of any kind.

You can only enrich the lives of others when you have enriched your own mind, and the only way you can enrich your own mind is to look it over. Cast out what you don't like, and expand what you do like.

WHAT IS YOUR PROGRAM GOAL?

When you discover that you do not have to live under the law of struggle and strain, you are halfway toward your program goal—no matter what it is.

Many people think only that they have to work hard for a living. They follow the world opinion and tell you how hard they struggle for a $102-a-week take-home pay or $164.21 take-home pay. Take-home pay is their only goal. They allot it according to their budget and as a result they get along. They have little freedom, but they get along, and by the time they pass on to the next phase of life, there is a nice stack of paid bills.

You don't need to be under that law if you remember

that you are a success-motivated person, and Divinely so. Make your self-image one of creativity.

A man who was a specialist, and worked in a consulting capacity only, told me that he worked about three days a month but got $2,000 a day for his work. Of course, he had in his consciousness trained abilities that were needed. He was not a high school dropout. He was a brilliant man, who, I am sure, had worked very hard many, many years, to achieve all that he knew. I'm certain that, on the days when he wasn't actually working, he was keeping up-to-date on the latest developments in his field.

People who, through their own correct self-recognition, are able to act as though things are so, are also able to make them so.

YOU CAN

I suppose that a hundred years ago they said you couldn't build the Panama Canal. But we have it because somebody said you can. You can use your creative abilities on any modern development from office buildings to new gimmicks and gadgets. This is because there are always success-motivated minds that do not believe it can't be done; people who aren't too tired, and aren't too busy, to see the possibility and ignore the probability.

Great creative ideas arrive in relaxed minds, and happen in relaxed minds. Once the ideas happen the person may have to use pressure. The person may have to use many man hours. But the idea comes in the relaxed attitudes when the success motivation has a chance to reveal itself.

In the old days the clergy would tell you to take time to be holy. All I can say to you is take time to relax.

A woman told me about her husband, who was a very productive man. "But he spends all of one day each week on the golf course," she said. "That's one of the reasons he is a success," I replied. You could do the same thing on a tennis court, or out fishing, or just walking down a country lane. Take time to let the creative ideas happen.

The success motivation in you, as you, wants expression, needs expression, and most frustrations are caused when the individual has not allowed the success motivation to function. They have lived in the *I can't do it* world. They have lived in the *I shouldn't* world. Any idea that tried to come through was quietly and definitely extinguished at the subconscious mind level.

I define success in this way: "Success is some form of creative production in life that is satisfying and expands the consciousness. Success is some kind of individual self-expression which is satisfying."

I'm not using the word *satisfying* to indicate resignation. Many people think they are satisfied with their way of living when they are not at all. They are resigned to ineffectual living.

Be a success in some form of life—and you need not become a millionaire. You may be a woman in the home, raising a family and running a good household. That's a success. You may be a woman with a professional career, or a beautiful flower garden. You may be a taxi driver who loves to drive cabs. You may be a farmer who loves to farm. These people are not resigned people. They are productive people who have satisfaction in what they are doing.

Satisfaction—a sense of accomplishing—that is what your success mechanism moves toward. A sense of well-being, a sense of being more than a body that needs to be fed, washed, and clothed. If you have a feeling of output other than just the strain and struggle of a busy existence, then you are what you were intended to be. You have mastered your success mechanism and put it to the right use.

CHAPTER

III

YOU ARE A
POTENTIAL

—

No one has ever seen the Divine power within you, but it is there. You are inward mind action, and as this action, which is able to control your experiences, you are invisible.

One of the great spiritual statements of all time—one of spiritual mysticism that is far beyond the limitations of religion—is a pronouncement of inward mind action: "I will lift up mine eyes unto the hills, from whence cometh my help."

The mystic has always known, what the layman has not known, that these words express an action of the mind. It is not lifting up the physical eyes, the outer sight. It is rather realizing that within your own consciousness, or mind, is the answer to your problem, no matter what that problem may be.

When you are in your usual concentration on your problem, and not recognizing that the solution lies within you, the mystic thinks of you as being down in the valley. But when you lift your consciousness from the problem to the solution, you have lifted up your mind unto the hills from whence cometh your help, for, it says, "My help cometh from the Lord," meaning from the inner spiritual resources of your own soul.

When I speak of lifting up my eyes, I am reminded of a story that I heard years ago. It dealt with one of the early saints of the church. There was one by the name of John, who plowed his field, and at the end of every furrow he would pause and look up for about thirty seconds. Then the plow would go down and make the next furrow. At the end, again, John would pause and look up.

Someone watching this performance asked the plowman why he did this. He replied that every downward look should be balanced with an upward look. I think this is what we do whenever we of the New Thought Movement get together. We look up, to start our minds again in a new direction. We remind ourselves of the wholeness and the completeness of life, and that there is a larger viewpoint.

YOU ARE MIND UNFOLDING

When I write of you as a potential, I am referring to the fact that inside the finished individual there is always the incomplete, unfinished, evolving mind. It matters not your age level. It matters not your situation. You are a movement of consciousness. You are mind unfolding itself. You always have been, you are now, and you always will be.

While consciousness acts through body, it is never body. It is mind and emotion. It is cause. It is the Creative Process.

The Infinite without the finite would never be complete. What good is a magnificent lake, a forest, an ocean, a mountain, or a valley if no one can see it? What good is the universe without an observer? You are the observer, but you are more than an observer. You are a participant. You are that which can create. All other forms of life create instinctively, and in minor ways. The beaver creates his dam. The bird builds its nest, and the lion adapts a special place for its lair.

But this is not creation as a Creator would want creation. This is not creation as a Creative Intelligence would schedule, plan, design, and formulate that which is forever new. So out of necessity for Its own self-expression It created you.

The great classic statement of this is the first chapter of Genesis, including the first two verses of the second chapter. These statements are symbolic. They are allegorical. They are the statement that the Creative Spirit, Mind, whatever It is, created a universe out of Itself and then created man in Its own image and Its own likeness to participate in the creation.

When this took place, no man or woman will ever know. It is a theory, but to me it is the answer: that you and I are alive in order to participate in the creative process.

YOU THE CREATOR

When I talk with people, I find that a large percentage of them do not believe that there actually is a reason for their being alive other than a biological one. They think of themselves merely as a biological happening, and often say that they did not ask to be born. They believe they are born to live out a lifespan between the date on their birth certificate and on their death certificate and that is all.

However, I believe that behind every person there is a plan and a purpose. There is a reason that is great. I do not believe that the Infinite Spirit, which we call God, could ever create by accident. When we are told that we are made in the image and likeness of the Infinite Mind, that is a way of saying that there is a magnificence possible to the individual.

If you are attuned to such thinking you will be aware of what Life is saying to you, which is: I created you. I equipped you. I leave you free. You are the freedom of the Spirit.

If you have such self-awareness, it is time for you to *be about your Creator's business.* It is time to dismiss all fear of failure; it is time to negate all doubts about your capabilities. It is time to invite that new idea which will lead you on the road of individual greater self-expression.

Does that mean that you are going to burst into song, write enchanting poetry, or paint a masterpiece? No. It means that you will feel free to know what you want to do, and to do it. We have already discussed your success mechanism, which is your subconscious mind doing what your conscious mind instructs it to do.

You may not realize it, but you already have been creating all your life, regardless of your belief in yourself or in anyone else, and you will continue to create as long as you live. But is the thing that you are creating the thing that you want? The most ineffective person that you know is creating something, if it is nothing more than a dull and drab existence. Unconsciously, that must be what he or she wants, in spite of the many complaints each makes. It is wise for you gradually to move such people out of your life. Let them function with other people like themselves, and ask, as Jesus did in a parable, "Can the blind lead the blind? Shall they not both fall into the ditch?"

This quote refers to the spiritually blind, those who keep their eyes and thoughts closed to their own potential. I am definitely not referring to the sightless in today's world. We all are aware of the remarkable performances of blind men and women who, through training and their own volition, live normal, productive, and happy lives.

When we know that we are creators, and *really* know it, then we assume the responsibility that goes with it and we produce for ourselves what we want. Most people have a list of what they want, but they do not realize that what they want has to come as a result of their own mind action. They want it to come from someone else. They want it to come from some external situation, condition, or individual.

Think for the moment of the creation of the railroad, the creation of the tallest building in the world, the longest bridge, or what you consider the greatest work of art, the finest drama, or the most fascinating book. You do not need to look to the past for tremendous creative achievements. They are all around you; everywhere for you to see. Each of these things has been, and is now, because some man or woman originated them in his or her mentality.

If anyone has originated in his or her mentality what

he or she wanted, then you can originate what you want in your mentality. Here is where most people back away. They say he can do it, or she can do it, but I can't do it. So they don't do it. Luckily science has come along and made us comfortable anyway. If you let everyone create for you, you can get the benefit. But that's such a waste of livingness and its joys.

As I mature, I am aware that there are areas in my own experience where I am not living enough. I am living in part, but not in full. As a matter of fact, most individuals are living only about forty per cent of the life they could live. A great teacher said that he came that we might have an abundant life, and every individual is endowed by right of being with the totality of life. The totality of life and its principle is one of expression, but most people use it as a law of repression.

REPRESSION AND EXPRESSION

When your grandparents and your parents wanted you to be a fine, good person, they surrounded you with repressions. Don't do this. Don't do that. Such repressions, if followed through to an extreme, may have led to neurotic states which either influenced the individual detrimentally in later life or had to be dealt with through corrective therapy.

There have been teachers who have followed the *you shouldn't* and the *you can't* line of thinking. But they were not great spiritual minds. They may have been great theological minds, but not spiritual minds. A spiritual mind is always an expression mind. Do this and you will prosper.

Do this and you will be made whole. Do this and the good will come to you. Everyone of the great prophets has been a *Do This* teacher, meaning *express, project, release, become.* We are not interested in the people who have said that virtue alone is its reward, or that poverty is indicative of a state of blessedness. There have been false messiahs down through the ages who said such things, but I do not believe them.

Many people find it simple merely to sit back and say there is nothing I can create. There is. Even if it is only to create a disturbance.

A man was in my office some time ago, and I asked him when was the last time that he lost his temper. "Oh," he said, "It must be thirty years ago." He sounded so pleased with himself. So I said, "You'd better go out and do it. It's about time you lost your temper." He couldn't understand my attitude. "I trained myself all my life on that score," he told me. Then I explained that he had trained himself into repression; that his emotions needed expression. I could also see that he hadn't laughed in a long, long time. He had steeled himself so that he could never shed a tear. This man was a walking robot. I felt certain that he couldn't love. He could not let himself go. In spite of this, he was a successful businessman—probably one whom all of his employees disliked. He was the head of a household, with a wife and children, whom, I suspect, he tried to repress into a mold similar to his own.

While we are told that we are created in the image and likeness of our Creator, and I believe that is true, most of us are initially patterned according to the image and the likeness of mother and father. Sometimes this is very good.

Sometimes it is not. If you find yourself filled with frustration, or repressed in any way, you needn't necessarily go out and have a temper tantrum. But face it squarely and know that what you lack in your life is self-expression. Maybe your childhood is partly to blame, but certainly you need to do some repair work on your present livingness.

Remember that you are a creator. You don't need to stay the way you are if you don't like yourself, or if you believe other people don't like you. Look at yourself in the mirror and admit that in some way it is your own fault. It is a reflection of the fact that there is something wrong with your own self-image. To be a creator, you do not need to create something large or something magnificent. Create something new in your life, even if it is only redecorating a room in your home or apartment. Create a new experience. Create new friends. You can do it, and if you keep trying, eventually you will find that you have created *a new you.*

IT TAKES EFFORT

The moment you are not purposefully creating something, your mind is bound to go into a reverse action. Your reaction may be worry, listlessness, or a sense of "what's the use?" Your mind goes at exactly the same speed constantly. In your waking hours you never cease thinking. You don't think quickly sometimes and think slowly at other times. Therefore, it is wise to know what your thoughts are. Give direction to them. Your capacity for thinking is the spiritual essence of life. When you are not giving it creative drive, and when you are not giving it creative expectancy, this wonderful mental capacity is likely to produce nothing more than an average experience. Repeated lack of direction can only produce an average life.

Furthermore, when you let your thinking go its merry way, the result probably will be depression, a multiplicity of negatives, a dress rehearsal of past hurts. Your mind, operating without conscious direction, may go to the past in order to avoid the present, or to avoid considering the future. Old memories are not very stimulating if they are filled with failures, disappointments, and I-wish-I-had speculations. Healthy memories of great experiences are quite different. They have value.

Directing thought and having conscious control is not always easy. You can't do it twenty-four hours a day, or even the major portion of the day. But you can make the effort, at least for limited periods of time. Exert the energy because there is no place for mental laziness in a world where you expect to have health, prosperity, love, and self-expression.

There is a grand design to life. There is a magnificent overall plan to being. This is what the great men and women have seen and proclaimed. This is what they have symbolized. This is what they have told their followers they could do. But most of the time the followers said, in effect, you do it for me.

When the multitudes following Jesus were hungry, they had made no provisions for food. Jesus fed them twice. But there is no record that he fed them after that. I think that in essence he said: "All right, I fed you yesterday and

I fed you today. From here on go to work. Feed your-
selves." There is nothing in the teaching of this man that
inspired laziness. There is nothing in the teaching of New
Thought that says you can have what you want without
doing anything to get it. This is not a get-rich-quick
scheme nor is it an instant success-without-effort program.

It is a science which says that you are a Divine creation.
You are a spiritual being that can conceive ideas. You are
a mind that not only can conceive ideas but can translate
them into form, and you will get the result of your ideas
after you have translated them into form. There is no such
thing as life living itself without effort, and any great
thing you have ever done, you did because you selected
to do it. You thought of yourself as doing it. You conceived
the finished result in your mind and you proceeded to
bring it to pass.

For instance, I know a number of men and women who
know how to make money and make it honestly. They expect to make it. They consider themselves making it. In
their own minds they image the finished action. And they
make money. Don't sit around wishing that you were like
them, wishing that you had their ability. Develop the
ability to do whatever you want. Develop it and put it to
work.

When you think about your desires for daily living, and
for your long-range program, there is one I hope you will
not forget. That is to have some fun. We all need more
fun in our lives, and by that I mean even frivolous fun.
Fun with good judgment. Fun with a good standard of
morals and ethics, but fun. You are a creator, so why
don't you make the decision to create the kind of joy you

want, the kind of fun you really enjoy, and the kind of fun you can share with those you love?

PROGRAM YOURSELF

We live in a world of automation; a world where many major office procedures are handled by computers. There are advertisements in the classified sections of all major newspapers, seeking young men and women who wish to be trained in the art of programming these computers. When you program a computer, you feed in facts, or information, manipulate certain parts of the mechanism, and let the machine come up with its solution to the problem that needs to be solved.

This procedure can be applied to your conscious and subconscious mind. You can, and should, program your *self* each day. Many of us find that using the first half-hour after awakening for this purpose is a useful habit. Others say they prefer to do their programming at night, and I know one man who says he always awakens at four o'clock in the morning to program his own mind for the coming day. When I asked him why he chose such an hour, he replied that the thoughts of most of the people in his area of the world were still then—inoperative because they were asleep—and so there was a minimum of interference from what we call the collective mind.

There has been some confusion about what we mean, in our field of thought, by programming. We definitely do not mean to sit down and make a list of all the things that have to be done during the business day, or during the sixteen hours that the average person will be awake.

We mean a spiritual programming; setting your self in tune with the Divine plan of the universe. We mean feeding into your subconscious mind the thoughts and emotions that will result in a greater understanding of you, and a clear acceptance of your capabilities. We mean a renewed acceptance of the fact that the world is created by a Divine Intelligence and that we are in it as that Intelligence individualized. We are in it as thinking, feeling, creating, expressing people. We are in it to live with wisdom and joy.

When you program your self—your subconscious mind —you will state clearly what your desires are; you will take time to visualize them and to accept them as being accomplished. You may say, "Here is a negative that I don't want in my life any more. Subconscious mind, erase it for all time. But here is a positive that I do want. I am going to produce it."

You will recognize that what I have been saying in a simple outline form is what we call a scientific prayer or a spiritual treatment. The following, in more specific terms, is one that I wrote recently. It is applicable to a phase of thinking which I have called "I Am Fully Alive":

The action of the Infinite Mind is Life, and my life is that Life now. My consciousness is this action. My body is this action. All my affairs are this action. God's action in me, through me, and as me is total action. It is always perfect and complete. It is always vital and productive. It is always healthy and abundant.

At this split-second I am this perfect action of life. In my subconscious mind any and all patterns of in-

action are now neutralized. Old ideas do not govern me. Old negative habits are gone. I am a today individual in perfect now action. All right action is mine to meet every demand of this day. I accomplish all things in ease and in order.

I know what I need to know at the instant I need to know it. I do what I need to do at the instant I need to do it. I have what I need at the instant I need it. I praise this action of God which I individualize. It is my sufficiency.

As you become familiar with the technique of treatment, you will use your own words to express your own thoughts and emotions concerning the day that is just beginning. I recommend that during this half-hour of preparation for the events to come you also include some reading of the vast literature that exists in this field. From this you may find yourself inspired with some great new ideas.

When I am reading serious books—and I read many of them—I sometimes look at the book and say silently, "You, as I read you, are going to unfold some wonderful new depths in my own mind. You are going to give me new ideas which will stimulate other new ideas inside myself."

You can do the same thing if you are at a concert, an opera, a ballet, or a theater of any kind. That new idea that comes to you through seeing or hearing will stimulate creativity within yourself in some interesting, new, and fresh ways, if you consciously direct your subconscious to be awake and aware to such possibilities. This is programming the self at times during the day or evening which are not set aside specifically for that purpose. But we must ever be alert to the vast opportunities we have for expanding our capabilities of self-expression.

Often when I am teaching classes I have the students take the two words I AM and put their full attention on just these two words for thirty seconds, or perhaps a full minute. I ask them not to relate these words to body or profession, or to the immediate situation. They are to think exclusively I AM and nothing more. Try it in the quiet of your own home. As I often say, that which I am is not name and number. It is unconditioned and free. That is what you are contemplating. You are contemplating the essence of being, and that is what the great spiritual thinkers, both East and West, did.

These great minds have taken a moment, or a few moments, on a disciplined basis, to deal with that which they were which was not name or profession; which while it used body was not body; and which, while it used intellect was not intellect. They were dealing with Pure Cause before it became Effect. You are always cause becoming effect. That is why your mind creates out of itself. That is why your emotions create out of themselves; whether it be a gracious home, a family, or a great business enterprise. By means of the individual, cause is always becoming effect.

It has been encouraging, during recent months and years, to note how many people, many of them young men and women, have become involved in the process of meditation. This no doubt has come about because of our troubled times, and troubled though they may be, they have not been without their therapeutic effect.

World conditions, disordered times, and a certain amount of progress in living have made people think about themselves. They are making people think about themselves individually and not collectively. That is what we are doing in our New Thought efforts. Everything begins and ends in the mind, the consciousness, of the individual. The only cause, medium, and effect—or cause, process, and result—is the consciousness of the individual.

Too many people have been putting power out into the world where it is not. If your consciousness is the same mind that was in Isaiah, Jesus, Paul, St. Augustine, or any of the others you want to name, including Plato, you are going to ask how you can improve so you can know it. You don't have to improve, you only need to know it.

You don't need to change the external of your life in order to know something in your mind. You do not awaken to your real potential through an external action. You awaken to it by correct individual knowing.

Take time for correct self-appraisal, as has already been suggested when we considered programming the self. Get correct self-recognition based on the truth that you are pure, unconditioned cause forever in the process of becoming effect.

When a great teacher said, "Go into your closet and shut the door," I am sure that he meant go into your mind. Take your attention off the world, off your individual world and the collective world. Begin to explore the depths. No wonder it has been said that the kingdom of heaven is in man, because those depths on the inside of consciousness are the most satisfying, the most refreshing that you will ever know.

They are the key to achieving your potential.

CHAPTER

IV

DISCOVER YOURSELF

You are spiritual, and the spiritual nature in man, which is the real self, is invisible.

The Infinite is always dealing with that which awakens, that which glimpses, that which sees, that which tastes and touches the freshness of life. Just as a diamond is many-faceted, forever flashing in a different way with every change of light that comes upon it, you and I are many-faceted individuals. We are largely unexplored territory of the Spirit. Medical men have told us about our physical selves, psychologists have told us some of the reasons why they believe we behave as we do, and theologians have often tried to apprise us of our errors, but you and I still don't know ourselves very well. This is wonderful, this is great, because within us we have the Divine urge to explore.

We know that we are vital centers of creativeness, and that we are not insignificant little people. So let's start our self-exploration with the premise that we are giants walking tall, with the light of the Spirit, with the Mind of the Infinite, with the emotions of Infinite Love, and let us know that we are the glory of Life Itself.

This is not an overestimation of what you and I really were created to be, but we must *realize* it and *accept* it as an ideal concept toward which we should direct our attention and toward which we can progress step by step. If we are to think of ourselves correctly, we should not think in limited, material terms.

THE IDEAL CONCEPT

It is never too early to develop this concept, in spite of the reaction of one mother on the West Coast who sent her little boy to one of our Sunday schools. The mother did not attend church, but when her son came home, she asked him, "What did you learn?" He said that all the children had recited over and over again, "Wonderful, wonderful me. I am made in the image and likeness of God." The mother was furious. She went to the telephone and called the clergyman, demanding to know why they were teaching such nonsense to children. "I think it is terrible," she said. But the clergyman replied, "I think it is wonderful."

To the mother, her son was just flesh and blood running around, and like all children, he frequently was annoying. But the instruction was correct. I believe that you and I might have faced many situations in life differently if we had started out with the concept of "Wonderful, wonderful me. I am made in the image and likeness of perfect Life."

Instead, we were told that children should be seen and not heard. We were told that we were naughty, bad, and if we didn't watch out one of our parents would report us to the corner policeman. It depended upon where you lived and your particular background, but you always got the threats.

The fact is that you and I are the ultimate of the Creative Process. We are the Creative Mind in action. When we take on this attitude about ourselves, we begin to see that we are wonderful. The individual is the magnificence of the Infinite Mind.

If you think in these terms, is there a tendency to find yourself in deep mental arguments because your whole reasoning mind has believed since the beginning of time that the exact opposite is true? The whole belief of the collective subconscious of the universe is the opposite of the statement "I am the magnificence of a Divine Mind."

THE REALLY SO AND THE APPARENTLY SO

It becomes obvious that as you go along in this teaching you have to decide what is really so and what is apparently so. There is a great difference between the two. Your depth of spiritual potential is really so. You can ignore it, you can deny it, and you need never think about it again. It still remains so. Perhaps you will instinctively turn to the apparently so, which is saying that man is born to suffer and man is born to die, but there is no other purpose for his being.

A truth which we can all accept is that you and I started as consciousness on a pathway of expansion which is always expanding. Your consciousness is greater today that it was a week ago, because you have been putting ideas into it for seven days. You have had seven days of believing something, and whether it was positive or negative, it has its expanding effect on your consciousness.

I believe that the Biblical statement "God hath made man upright; but they have sought out many inventions" tells a lot about all the inhabitants of the earth. The first part, *God hath made man upright*, refers to man collectively. The second part, *but they have sought out many inventions* refers to men as individuals. Man actually sought out these inventions because he had been taught to discredit himself, to consider himself a no-good sinner who would be lucky if he didn't land in hell. He couldn't really believe that he was wonderful, or even potentially wonderful.

One of the inventions that started as far back as recorded history, and even farther back, is the invention of two separate powers—one is good and one is evil. Do you believe that there is a power of evil that can and supposedly does operate? Then you are believing what is only an apparent truth. It comes in very handy because it explains all the negatives and all the unpleasant or seemingly catastrophic events in your life.

We say that there is One Mind which is all power. Man himself has created all the evil there is by misusing the power of Mind. No gun has ever shot itself off. No bottle of whiskey has ever opened itself. You can go on endlessly with illustrations. Wherever there are negatives, individuals are involved. So one of the many inventions is this *not so* truth of the two powers.

Another invention is the belief that in order to get any-where in this world you have to fight. You have to tread over others. You have to use devious ways. That's an ap-parent truth, but it is not so. It is merely a false conclusion believed by millions and used by millions.

A negative belief is not a truth. It is a false concept of a truth. A truth is that there is one Power, one Presence, one Mind, one Cause, and we are free to use it any way we want to use it. Sometimes we learn through disastrous ex-perience that our use has been a mistaken idea of what course of action we should take. We have not depended on the inner guidance that is always available to us at every instant of the day or night.

WHAT SHOULD YOU ACCEPT?

You and I, as adults, have been told by one of the great teachers of wisdom that we need to become as little chil-dren. We are told to *accept the thing as being so.* But that does not mean a thoughtless acceptance of what the world or some individual tells us. The prophet of two thousand years ago referred to well-thought-out desires, which, he told those who listened to him, would be true according to their belief.

Many children believe in Santa Claus because their parents tell them the jolly old man exists. This is a harm-less belief of childhood, when the parent is the fount of wisdom, the fount of authority. As adults, however, we should not accept a thing as authority without investi-gating it. We should not accept ourselves as mortal or as average human beings, because that is not what we were created to be.

By knowing what you are, you know what you are not. You know that as the magnificence of a Creative Mind you are not subject to the ills, or to the problems of the race, or the group in which you function.

Each day you are likely to be faced with one or several untruths and expected to believe them. You have your own set of balances—your own thoughts and emotions. Use them to weigh the evidence. Then remember that you can always change what you believe when you have decided to change it.

Often this will require considerable effort. Some of the old beliefs that we have are bound by roots that go down, down, down into the subconscious mind, and they are very hard to uproot. Some of them have been nutured for years. The business of trying to dismiss them is not easy. It takes definite, specific work, starting with intention and decision, followed by careful watching of your mental attitudes.

Let's take the simple matter of happiness and unhappiness. I believe you were born to be happy, but often you awaken and say, "I am unhappy." You may or may not know the reason for your depression. Nevertheless you face it, clear it, and finally let it work itself to its conclusion. Balance is restored and you are happy again. The unhappiness is the apparently so and happiness is the real truth. Similar examples can be made concerning self-confidence and lack of self-confidence, freedom from guilt and guilt feelings, or financial ease and lack of financial ease.

The list of truths and apparent truths which occur in

your life may be entirely different from those in mine. They may seem very difficult to master, but a change from the negative to the positive is always possible when you recognize that all power exists at the center of your being.

When you review your self-image, and really face up to the way you rate yourself, never let discouragement overtake you. Here are some truths that you can say aloud, or silently, and accept as applying to you. *I am spiritual. I am creative. I do not fit into all patterns. I am original. I am unique.* This will help to break the old patterns, the old inventions, many of which you probably created yourself.

Occasionally, in consultation work, I have said to a person, "You are a spiritual being." The statement comes as a jolt. The individual is almost frightened of the word. He doesn't really want to believe he is spiritual, because he is bound by tradition. He doesn't want to believe it because of the responsibility that goes with it. If you assume that you are spiritual you can't go around being stingy, rude, inconsiderate, or unkind. The word spiritual has a confusing meaning because of the way it has been used in the past. Some people believe it means sanctimonious or holier-than-thou. So let's make some substitutions to our earlier statements and say, *I am Creative Cause. I am expression. I am a thinker who thinks greatly. I am an emotion which loves greatly.*

A HEALTHY MIND

Any mind, in order to be healthy, has to be an expressive mind. It cannot be a frustrated mind. As an expressive mind, it has to create out of itself. The basis of life from the highest point of view is that of a sound mind.

A statement which I call one of spiritual psychology was made by Paul. Perhaps these words are familiar to you: "God hath not given us the spirit of fear; but of power, and of love, and of a sound mind." You and I, in order to have a sound mind, need to give of ourselves, and I am not speaking of money or charity. I'm speaking of giving yourself away, and you can only give yourself away through communication with people. They don't always have to be present. You could write a letter to someone with whom you wanted to share your self-expression. You could make a telephone call. Communication with others can take many forms, but you have to give yourself away. Your consciousness is the only real thing you have to give, and when you give yourself away, you are actually giving to yourself. You are profiting by the experience.

You should give away a sound mind. Therefore, you do not give away your fears. You do not give away your troubles. You do not give away your problems or your frustrations. Find the answer to your unhappiness or bitterness in your own mind, where there is always a solution. Don't foist unpleasantness or personal despair on others.

How many times in the last week have you talked with a friend and not told your troubles? Whom have you talked with on the phone and not disclosed your problems or your anxieties? How many people can say that they contacted you this week, met you, talked with you, or received a letter from you that displayed a sound mind?

William James, the great philosopher and psychologist

of Harvard University, called our teaching "The Religion of Healthy-Mindedness." In his book *The Varieties of Religious Experience* (1902), he predicted that ours would be one of the new creative ideas in the field of religion, and it has been.

CONSCIENCE—YOUR OWN CREATION

One of the most delightful things about modern psychology is that in the last fifty years its researchers have discovered that your conscience is your own creation and you can't go by it at all. You don't have a guilty conscience; you just have guilt. The reason you don't do certain things isn't because Infinite Mind gave you a conscience. It is because, somewhere along the way, you built that conscience so you wouldn't do certain things. You may have done it to please your mother. You may have done it to please your father or your Sunday-school teacher. You may have done it to please any number of people, or to meet certain situations or events, but you have built your own conscience.

In the old days we believed that the criminal went against his own conscience. He doesn't go against his own conscience at all. His conscience agrees with what he is doing. The man who consistently robs doesn't sit up nights worrying about it. He sits up nights figuring out who to rob next. The professional gambler doesn't worry when he takes the last dollar from his opponent. He goes home and sleeps very well, gets up the next day, and figures out whom he can play that night to get more money. He has no conscience, and you have no conscience except the one you have created. You have no monitor to your mind except your own creation. You have no guard that stands at the portal of your thought save yourself.

It is true that there are many things you do not allow yourself to think. There are many emotions that you do not allow yourself to express. There are guards and gates that you have put up around your mind. This you must do in order to live in our society. This is good as long as it does not inhibit or frustrate you. Nevertheless nothing goes out from you save that which you are giving to yourself, because you are the alpha and the omega; the beginning and end of all your experience.

This explains the importance of the symbol of Infinite Mind leading Abraham to the top of a mountain, in Genesis, and saying: "Lift up now thine eyes, and look from the place where thou art northward, and southward, and eastward, and westward: For all the land which thou seest, to thee will I give it, and to thy seed for ever"; the meaning being, your entire experience is yourself.

All of your experience is an extension of yourself. Your office is an extension of yourself; your home is an extension of yourself; your friendships are extensions of yourself; and your love for people is an extension of yourself. No one can love you until you can love yourself, and you cannot love anyone else until you love yourself.

BE GLAD YOU ARE IMPERFECT

If we were perfect we would have nothing to do. This would be the dullest universe that anyone ever could be in. Just imagine if you were perfect, if you never thought anything unkind and never did anything wrong. Just imagine if no one else ever did anything wrong and the government was perfect.

Be glad you are imperfect and that you make mistakes. That means you still have something to do. There are accomplishments ahead of you and they are necessary for your unfoldment. You live on the basis of expectation and so do I. That's what keeps you alert and on the go. People who have nothing to look forward to are sad people; they are desolate people because they have abandoned hope. As long as you have hope, you have life. As long as you have hope you have a creative mind with creative interests.

I believe that every mistake any person makes is absolutely necessary for that person to make. It is part of the learning and evolving process. I believe we go through the experience of evil in order to know its opposite, just as we go through the changing seasons and learn to appreciate the beauties and understand the vicissitudes of each. We need variety in our livingness as we move our incomplete selves toward greater perfection.

There are many people who lead monotonous lives and are devoid of all inspiring thoughts or activities. Beware of monotony. It is the death experience. It is a killer. It is a disease. As you know, in our teaching we are not concerned with disease of the body. We are concerned with that which breathes infection into the mind. When we have a well mind, we have a well body. Monotony is the infection we must all avoid! Keep it at a minimum each day, because it is destructive. When life becomes monotonous you tend to think that you have gone as far as you can go. That is not true. No person on earth has gone as far as he can go.

The Infinite is always evolving itself and you and I are in this Creative Process, moving forward step by step as we realize what we are and know what to do next.

Many years ago, when this teaching originated, between 1875 and 1900, the early teachers took as their statement the one from the Sermon on the Mount which says: *Ye shall be perfect, even as your Father in heaven is perfect.* They premised their teaching on *Perfect God, Perfect Man,* and *Perfect Being.* You will find this taught in the early New Thought literature. The whole teaching concerned a perfect person, in a perfect state, in a perfect process. These early teachers did not realize that when you give a person too great an ideal, you have many who cannot accomplish it. Therefore, you have the problem of guilt increased rather than diminished.

We have not abandoned the ideal, but it is an ideal just as *peace on earth and good will to men* is an ideal. We have the ideal in order to move toward it, even though at the present time it is not possible, nor was it possible when Jesus was born, or when Emerson was born, or when you were born. It isn't possible for children who are born today. But without the ideal we would not progress. You and I are moving forward toward greater self-expression, which may be all that Ultimate Perfection is.

CHAPTER

V

YOUR INHERENT
WISDOM

—

You are born in the Infinite Wisdom. The totality of know-how since time began is available to you, and as you learn to draw upon this Infinite knowledge you expand your consciousness, but your inner self remains invisible.

Occasionally, in my capacity as a clergyman, I am called upon to christen a newborn child. I use a simple ceremony which does not include baptism, because I believe every person is born pure. As I look at the baby, usually about six weeks old, I marvel at this spontaneous creature. So far no limitation has been enforced upon it. Here is something of Life, not yet restricted, not yet inhibited and not yet neurotic. Being aware of this child's potential, I wonder how it will develop; what its future will be. Perhaps its self-realization will be in the arts, in science, in space navigation, in social service, or in some as-yet-undreamed-of accomplishment. The baby's self-expression and resultant happiness may involve homemaking, office work, or rearing a family. The important question is: Will the Creative Process be given the chance to operate fully in this new individual as he or she goes through the normal procedures of growing up and maturing?

We know that in this little body there is a mind, a subconscious and a conscious mind, which will develop along with the child. This infant, like all infants throughout the world, is born in wisdom—the Infinite Wisdom in which we believe.

THE UNIVERSAL SUBCONSCIOUS

For many years our teaching pioneered. We said that the subconscious mind was the Mind of the Universe, and that in it was the total wisdom of all past experience from the dawn of time. We said that this wisdom is in every individual's subconscious mind. There were many critics who did not accept our belief.

Then there rose into prominence a Swiss psychiatrist, Carl Gustav Jung, whose name is well known in the field of psychotherapy and to many laymen. One of the ideas he developed has been called the theory of *collective unconscious*. In it he worked out the concept that the individual unconscious mind exists in a total unconscious mind, is a form of it, and that this total unconscious mind contains the collective experience of all the individuals from the dawn of time.

This is much the same as what I have said about our belief, which we held before Dr. Jung's disclosure of his theory. However, Ernest Holmes, founder of this instruction, disagreed with the Jungian concept in one respect, and he made this very clear in his textbook, *The Science of Mind,* and in other writings. We hold that it is not a collective *unconscious,* as the psychiatrist proclaimed it, but it is a collective *subconscious,* the difference being that if it were unconscious it couldn't function as a source of Infinite Wisdom. An unconscious mind cannot perform the simplest tasks, but the subconscious mind is ever active, even in sleep.

You are in this collective or universal subconscious mind from the time of your birth. You come into this world as a part of the Infinite Wisdom of the ages. Whatever anyone has ever thought, felt, or experienced at any time, is in the universal subconscious mind ready to be known whenever it needs to be known by an individual. Haven't you occasionally been puzzled by a question, only to have the answer pop into your mind unexpectedly? Or perhaps you were intuitively guided to some book or magazine that contained the information you wanted.

Many people believe that a genius is a person who is able, in some intuitive way, to open up the great resources in his particular field of this collective subconscious knowing. If you are aware that this fund of knowledge is available to you, and accept the fact, you will find that ideas come to you; information comes to you in a surprising way.

This is why in the Book of Proverbs it says that we do not need to rely upon our own understanding. This is why a great teacher said that *the Father in me, he doeth the work,* meaning there is that in the individual which is capable of knowing whatever needs to be known at the instant of time that it needs to be known.

UNSUSPECTED RESOURCES

Dr. Brown Landone was a well-known figure in our field of thought back in the thirties and forties. He had been a medical doctor before he came to the New Thought work, and he was a prominent writer and lecturer for many years. Brown Landone was born into a wealthy family in Philadelphia, over a hundred years ago, and was always known as a sickly child who had to be nursed through one illness after another.

When he was about thirteen, something happened that started the boy thinking in a new way. Prior to this time he had had nurses around the clock. They got him up, dressed him, and led him to a chair. He sat there while he ate a simple meal and as soon as it was finished a nurse got him back into bed for a nap. Young Brown lived the usual routine of an invalid.

One day, when he and a nurse were alone in the house, the nurse discovered that a bottle of the boy's special medicine was empty. She asked him if he would be all right while she went to the drugstore some distance away. He assured her that he would.

When the nurse had been gone less than five minutes, Brown began to smell smoke and knew that something was on fire. He remembered that his father had instructed the servants concerning one important thing they must do if ever the house caught fire. He had told them that a metal chest in the attic contained every valuable paper he possessed. They were to get that metal chest out.

The boy, with the smell of smoke in his nostrils, could think of nothing but the metal chest. He was not aware of the events that followed his concerned thoughts until he found himself standing on the sidewalk beside the precious box. He suddenly realized that he, the supposed invalid, had gone to the attic, two floors above his bedroom and five floors from the street. There he had picked up the heavy chest and carried it to the sidewalk. When he came to the realization of what his subconscious mind had caused him to do, he fainted dead away.

The fire was extinguished without any great harm and the nurse prepared to put the young patient back in bed. He refused to go. "I want to sit in this chair and think," he told her.

In later years, when I knew the man well, he told me that at the time of the fire he had awakened to the fact that he had performed an extraordinary feat without any conscious awareness of it. If he could do that subconsciously when he was ill, he reasoned, he certainly could do it consciously. He decided that he was not going back to bed except to sleep at night, and he never did.

Brown Landone, the mature man, was perfectly well and happy until the end of his days. For years he had declared that he would pass on at the age of ninety-nine years and nine months, and that the event would take place at nine o'clock in the morning.

On that day he got up as usual and had everything in perfect order. At five minutes to nine he said to his secretary, "Come in and sit beside me. I'm going to lie down on the bed because I think I'll go on my way." At exactly nine o'clock the heart stopped and, on his own decision, Dr. Landone went over to the other side of life.

This man was robust when I knew him during the last

fifteen years of his life, and he was a noncomformist. He had been one ever since that long-ago day when subconsciously he drew upon his unsuspected physical resources. His mind knew that the box had to get down from the attic, and his body brought it down.

THE INFINITE KNOW-HOW

There are many stories of people who under emergencies are able to perform extraordinary acts of strength or endurance, but I do not, at this time, intend to refer particularly to physical feats. I am referring to the great depths in you and in me that are there from the beginning of time. I know, for instance, that I have within me the history of every nation that has ever been. I don't need to have all of that particular knowledge in my profession, so I do not draw extensively upon it. However, if I were a professional historian—a university professor of history —I could open up great depths of historical knowledge within myself. The same would be true in any other profession or field of endeavor.

Perhaps you have had the experience of being in an unfamiliar place, yet feeling that you have been there before. Psychologists call this phenomenon *déjà vu* and explain it in various ways. People who believe in reincarnation say that you have actually been there before in another incarnation. We, however, consider this experience another manifestation of the individual's ability to tap the universal fund of knowledge.

I recall that about twenty years ago we were planning to hold a ten-day seminar in upstate New York, at Lake

Minnewaska. My then·associate minister and one of the secretaries had gone up to see the place. They reported its beauty and said I must see it. I agreed, so we drove up and I was taken to the hotel we planned to use. It stood high on a cliff's edge beside the lake. As I viewed the remarkable scene, I felt that I had been there before. Later, when I got out on the trails and roads, I was absolutely at home. This pleases the reincarnationists, who say I *have* been there before, but I have to remind them that the hotel is less than one hundred years old.

I believe that as I stood there my subconscious mind, being part of the universal subconscious mind, made me feel at home, because it was able to anticipate the pleasant fifteen-year experience that was to follow, as we held our annual seminars at Minnewaska for that length of time. Knowledge of the lake and its surroundings had been in my subconscious mind all the time. Some action in my intuitive nature had opened my conscious mind to the entire scene, making it seem familiar.

Most people who have such experiences don't think very much of them when they happen. But you can quite often recollect them later, when a trapdoor in your mind opens up and that which always has been in you suddenly is in front of you.

Take this thought into your consciousness: *The total know-how of all time is in me and it doeth the work. I do not have to lean upon my own understanding, because if I lean only on what my intellect has absorbed, knows, and believes, I am living only a part of Life, a small fraction. The universal subconscious in me is a storehouse of past, present, and future experiences.*

YOUR MIND IS AT THE CENTER

Visualize with me the figure of an hourglass. It used to be common equipment in the kitchen and was used for timing such things as boiling an egg. It took a known number of minutes for the sand that filled the top half of the glass to filter down to the bottom half.

There is a distinct similarity between life and the hourglass. I like to think that the top section represents the totality of life, the totality of mind, the totality of know-how, and you and I are that point at the center through which the greatness and the magnificence of life filters into our individual experience. Your mind and my mind are at the center point, the filtering point, or perhaps we might call it the distribution point. How we distribute this totality of life, of mind, of know-how, and at what rate, depends upon our self-awareness and our intuition.

I have defined intuition as the spot where you and the Creative Process are one. Intuition stays at the idea level and does not deal with personalities. It is not to be confused with desire.

We exist in a tremendous arena of mind action: Call it Consciousness; call it, as Emerson did, the Oversoul; call it as Jesus did, Heaven. Whatever name you want for it is unimportant. Here is a wealth of intelligence that is seeking to filter through our minds and to flow out into our world.

You will recall the great sentence: *In earth as it is in heaven.* In that context we might think of the top section of the hourglass as heaven and the bottom section as earth. The Infinite is releasing intelligence so that which is perfect as idea can filter down and be perfect in form. This is why man has had the consistent hope, or shall we call it a dream, of the *kingdom of heaven on earth*; and the brotherhood of man. This has been taught for as long as we have had religion, and as far back as we can go in the study of man we find religion. There has always been that in man's nature which has wanted to feel that he is a part of a larger design, of a greater plan, of a wiser order.

Many religions have not survived because they have become archaic. Religions have become outmoded because they have become less and less helpful to the follower and more and more symbolic. New prophets, new teachers, new messiahs, and new saviors continue to arise. They are the forerunners of new religions. Great ideas have not stopped. The Infinite is always renewing Itself and releasing Itself by means of people.

Your mind is the point through which the Infinite filters into the finite. It is the place where unlimited ideas can be released. Whether they will be or not is another matter. They can be, because they are there. In your mind, right now, is what Peter called the *inheritance incorruptible*. In your mind, right now, are great intelligent ideas, billions of them, waiting to filter through your consciousness.

Many of you are going to say, "If this is so, why isn't my present earth (meaning home, job, family, social relations, and so on) a heaven?"

The answer is that you haven't let the ideas filter through, because you are mentally and emotionally congested and the point of distribution is clogged with doubts, fears, and false beliefs. Every once in a while, we consciously or uncounsciously clear up some of the congestion and let an idea flow through. Those of us who are trained in this spiritual science know exactly how to do it. We know how to give a spiritual mind treatment, an affirmative prayer, which decongests the congestion by uncovering and neutralizing the negatives that cause the obstruction.

Anything that clears your mind lets more of the Infinite intelligence flow through. As more Divine know-how flows through, you experience more prosperity, more ease and more joy in your world. There will be less harassment, less strain, and less struggle. Problems minimize as ideas come through.

The original reason for your having a mind cannot be so you can use it to worry, be anxious, and be disturbed. This would be ridiculous. Everything creative that has come to men and women has come when they have used the magnificent operation of mind and emotion in the right way.

Remember that there is an idea in your mind waiting to come into your world if you will decongest your mind. One of the great ways to do this is: *to know what you want, be certain that you will have it, and the idea will drop through the filter. Heaven will come to earth.*

The Infinite cannot withhold its Divine givingness. There is no way to restrict this Divine bounty except by the way you use your mind. If your life isn't going the way you want it to, you might take some time and list the six main worries that keep eating at you all the time. The only reason I suggest this is so you will face up to them and say, "What am I going to do about them?" That's the only virtue in it. These are points of congestion which are inhibiting you, limiting you. They don't need to be there. You can get rid of them. You don't need to have six worries in your life.

I find that I do not use the word *worry* very much any more. I use the word *concern*. Not long ago, on a wintry Sunday morning, I got the eight o'clock weather report. The temperature was fifteen degrees. I was concerned. There is nothing worse than standing on a platform, before a microphone and fifteen hundred empty seats. I am sorry to say that many of the members of my congregation have a belief in weather. They let it influence their activities, and I needed an audience.

What could I do? I sat down and said, "Clear your mind." I did just that. I reminded myself that the Divine Presence would be in Alice Tully Hall whether the congregation was or not. I reminded myself that there would be thousands of people listening to me on radio whether there was a congregation or not. With that I stopped. I no longer had any concern. That morning I had one of the best congregations of the entire season, and I wondered how many of those present had made their decision to be there at eight o'clock while I was clearing my mind.

You can clear your mind in just as simple and straightforward a manner. While your subconscious mind is handling all of the automatic actions of your daily life, your conscious mind can run riot. It can have a wonderful time being anxious. It can have a wonderful time bearing a grudge, hating the place where you work, or resenting some remark your neighbor made to you. Instead of rehashing the insults and hurts you believe you have to endure, either by mulling them over or by telling them to someone else, sit down and clear your mind of each and every one of those negatives. You may have to handle them one at a time, but be certain to handle them all eventually. Then watch the new, the creative, ideas come through. No one should ever be guilty of thinking or saying, "My life is just about the same as it has been for years."

THE IMPORTANCE OF CHANGE

Everything in the universe is in a constant process of change, and you have to be, too. I have to change constantly because everything around me is changing. Make a study of political history and see the rise and fall of empires, each one of them certain that it would be a power forever. I am certain that Queen Victoria believed the statement that the sun would never set on the British Empire. Many citizens of the United States are egotistical enough to believe that our present political structure will go on forever, and we will always be the richest country in the world. Other nations have different views and are altering their concepts of themselves and the roles they will play.

So much for the world we all live in, but what about yourself or some of your loved ones? I know people who, in spite of world progress, are trying to stand still. They are literally putting up their guards, their wall, their battlements so as not to change. This is an absolute refutation of Life itself.

Unless you are a changing individual in a changing experience, you are bound to become a congested individual.

Out of this congestion will come your illnesses, your problems, your difficulties, and your unpleasant situations. These things will not occur because they are necessary to you, but because you have created them by your own unconscious decision to stay the way you are. You become a static individual trying to maintain a static world, and it can't be done. Cracks eventually appear in your walls. They may appear as anything from arthritis to a broken marriage.

The persistence of the Infinite is magnificent. It never gives up. It waits until you and I take our own minds, our own emotions, and discipline them. It waits until we make changes in our attitudes.

You do not know it, but your mind is hungering and thirsting for something new—something different, something vital, something creative, and something triumphant. Is your subconscious mind, in its role as the doer in your success mechanism, asking this question: "Isn't this individual ever going to give me any new material?"

No matter what it is that you need, the idea of it is in your mind right now, waiting to come through. If you are sick, the idea born of the spirit of health is in your mind. But it can't come through as long as you recite the symptoms. If you have financial difficulties, the wealth of the universe is in the next idea in your mind which is trying to come through. Your congestion point of "I can't afford it" is standing in the way. I could go on with any negative situation which you might want me to discuss, and whatever it is the idea for the solution is in your mind this instant.

You have to redefine yourself as an inside person—an

invisible, not an outside, person. This instruction is not interested in your height, your weight, or the clothes you wear. These are outside details that you automatically take care of yourself. In fact, your subconscious mind does it for you. I'm talking about the inside—mind and emotion, thought and feeling, ideas old and new. I'm talking about the negatives with their destructive tendencies and the positives with their creative tendencies. All of the universe is saying: "Think something new, do something new, and be something new."

GUARD YOUR ATTENTION

Each of the wonderful accomplishments we have experienced in this world has been possible because somewhere some person intuitively opened up the wisdom of the ages. In this connection, there are those who will say that the entire record includes all the destructiveness that ever has taken place. This is true, and it is possible to draw upon destructive ideas as well as those that are constructive. I believe that the ideas come from where our attention is, and our whole philosophy is to keep our attention on the creative side of life. When we do this, creativeness comes forth.

Let's consider the friend, the loved one, who is always depressed. Where is his or her attention? For this person, out of the depths of the subconscious mind, there wells up the unhappiness of the human race. Often, at the intellectual level, the person has nothing to be depressed about. The problem is one of directing attention. The hypochrondiac needs to take his mind off his pills, and the

lonely individual needs to direct attention to a sincere
effort to find more friends.

Where your attention goes, there the ideas follow. This
no doubt is why Paul gave a long list of creative ideas and
at the end said: *Think on these things.*

"THE OUGHT TO BE IS"

I recall a Chinese proverb that I learned from a teacher
many years ago. She said, always remember this: "The
ought to be, is." At the time I thought it was rather foolish.
Through the years, however, that bit of philosophy has
brought me through many difficult situations. It is another
way of saying, "Whatever will be, already is," or "Believe
that you already have what you want, and you have it."

We are in a total mind and emotion in which all ideas
are past, present, and future. If you read about the beginning of any great advancement in industry or elsewhere,
you will find that uncongested people brought about the
new development. Frequently there were many people
working separately on the same idea, because each had
let it filter through from the universal source.

I'm thinking now of the development of the automobile.
We always think of Henry Ford in this connection, but
long before Mr. Ford there were hundreds of people, without any special knowledge of how to build an automobile,
yet who were busily building early models in small back-
yard shops. Each brought forth a know-how that had
never been known before. Later the competition and the
costs resulted in a consolidation of the industry.

There are minds many all in mind one. This is your inheritance. You do not earn it. It is free. You may learn and earn techniques by which to use the mind. The singer has to practice many hours a day. The dancer must do the same, and the executive in his office uses various methods of perfecting the ideas that come to him from the Infinite storehouse.

We have said that the newborn child is born into the immensity of mind. You and I, the disciplined adults, are still in the immensity of mind. We have a foundation which no man has ever seen, because the great principles, the great resources are not to be seen, but to be known. What any mind has ever known, you can know just by dwelling upon it.

CHAPTER

VI

PROFITABLE
THINKING

—

Prosperity is a spiritual value within you which is invisible until you demonstrate it.

When New Thought started, about one hundred years ago, the Movement was unique, and to some extent it still is, because our teaching clearly emphasizes that a person or a group of people can use a spiritual premise and have expanding prosperity in material goods. In those early days, this concept did not meet with the approval of the theological minds who praised the virtue of poverty and felt that the poor and neglected were the chosen of the Infinite. Today, however, most of the larger church organizations have accepted our idea in principle and no longer defame the rich and ennoble the poor.

The individual is his own prosperity. I am my own prosperity. You are your own prosperity. So let us defiine what we mean by that term. *Prosperity is the freedom to do what you want to do when you want to do it.*

Most people think of prosperity in terms of money.

Having all the money you need is very important. However, as you go along, you will find that such things as health, love, and creative ideas also play a part in the definition: Prosperity is the freedom to do what you want to do when you want to do it.

How do you achieve this freedom? Perhaps your earnings are low or you may even be temporarily unemployed. How do you go about achieving the prosperity that may seem far beyond your reach? You do it by what I call profitable thinking. By thinking what you want, you stop thinking what you don't want. Gradually, what you don't want slips away, and in its place that which you want begins to happen. We know that the subconscious mind takes what you give it, and produces it. One of the great things that we now understand is that the subconscious mind is totally impersonal. It is as impersonal as an egg-beater, which beats eggs but doesn't know that it is beating them. Your subconscious mind takes what you give it and assumes that what you give it is what you want.

Unfortunately, many individuals think anything that comes into their heads and don't expect results from that thinking. Suppose you sit down for an hour's session over your bills, which seem pretty steep to you, and at the end of the period you say, "I know God's prosperity will take care of me." Then you walk away from your desk. What do you think will happen?

The Universal Mind must, according to Its law, act upon your thoughts. Sixty minutes have been devoted to concern about money and about thirty seconds were given to leaving it up to Divine Cause. Prosperity cannot result from such unevenly balanced thinking. Your answer will be unprofitable, rather than profitable.

Your deliberate thinking—what I call your intention thinking—is a spiritual tool that you use to bring abundance into your life. You also use your feelings—your emotions—as you think with intent, with purpose, and with plan in order to cause any object or event that you desire to materialize. You can demonstrate only that which you hold steadfastly in your consciousness.

One thing is certain, however. You must know what you want. It is amazing to me that there are so many people in this world who do not know what they want. These are the people who often say, "Well, I'd like to . . ." or "It has always been my dream. . . ." I call these individuals the halfway people. They can express a hope in a halfhearted and unbelieving way, but they never say, "I *want* this" or "I *want* that." These halfway people, who are never sure, look like people who are either too afraid or too lazy to try. They are men and women of indecision. They never think in a decisive way. Their negative mind-action is unprofitable. It gets them nothing but frustration and more problems.

You cannot proceed a single step forward in your experience of prosperity without a clear-cut desire. Once you are completely aware that there is something you want, go after it by creating a self-image in which you already have what you want. Work unceasingly until you get the object you desire. It may be money, a new home, a new car, or a trip abroad. It may also be health and an ability to be more self-expressive.

CLARIFY YOUR DESIRE

Desire is the key to prosperous living. We all need money, and we need to think of it in larger terms than the day-to-day requirements. The need of money, and the use of money as a means of exchange, is a part of our economic system. It is essential and you *can* have it. Believe in it. Like it. I sometimes say, "I love my checkbook." This is possible because we have moved a long way from the time when money was called filthy lucre or the root of all evil.

I suggest that you take ten minutes, sit down, and think of nothing but prosperity. This may not be easy. You know all about the light and gas bill. You know all about the rent or the mortgage payments on your home. You can think about these, and do it frequently. Now think about money with the same great ease. Think about money in all of its forms. Look in your wallet and study the faces of the men who are on each of the bills. Make a point to learn the faces that are on each denomination of bill that forms a part of the United States currency. I particularly enjoy contemplating the one that bears the likeness of Ulysses S. Grant. Having a few of these can give you great freedom.

That's only one way of thinking about prosperity. Look about in your apartment or in your home and consider the things that cost the most. Say, "Aren't these wonderful?" Get out your jewelry and wear it. Eat tomorrow's breakfast with the sterling silver you keep for special occasions. It will never wear out. Watch your attitudes about your use of money and the valuable possessions that you are inclined to hoard instead of enjoying.

I remind myself several times a week that money is the action of Life in a specialized way for my freedom, for my enjoyment, for my ease, and it really is spiritual, not material. I believe that the demarcation between spiritual and material is something we have set up through the ages and it is time we dismissed it. There is no line of demarcation. Everything is spiritual and everything is fundamentally good. When it seems evil it is because of our human misuse of mind. This includes money, which is not merely a means of exchange, but a joy and a delight. It is wonderful in all forms—in accumulation, release, and spending. It makes for spiritual freedom, while debt always carries with it a neurosis.

Years ago, Ernest Holmes wrote an article entitled "God Loves a Prosperous Man." We were rather holy in those days, about thirty-five years ago, and many of the teachers in the field shook their heads. "Mr. Holmes has gone commercial," they said. Even I was a bit dismayed at the title, but gradually I got used to it, and finally I said, "That's good." It had become apparent to me that when a man or woman is prosperous—and that doesn't necessarily mean possessed of great wealth—he or she has a less cluttered mind. There is less cause for concern, anxiety, or fear. Therefore, Creative Cause can operate more fully through such a mind.

From that moment of clarification, I accepted a new self-image. I viewed myself as a prosperous man. Before that time, I had thought that money was something one collected in church, but never discussed unless it was necessary to ask for a new roof or an extra collection for Easter.

If you can accept yourself as prosperity and use that word, go one step further and say, "I am money in circulation." This statement may come as a shock to your subconscious mind, steeped as it is in the old traditions. However, when the subconscious knows you really mean it, and goes to work, things begin to happen.

If you have difficulty believing that you can truly be prosperous try saying these words repeatedly: *Within me there are plenty of talents. I now change my consciousness from one of poverty to one of prosperity.*

YOUR RECEPTIVITY

We know that whatever is Creative Cause, that which in the older days we called God and what today we call Mind, has always been beneficent. We know It has always been creating out of Itself and giving Itself away. This is why we have a cosmos. This is why we have every form of life that exists on earth. This is why man has evolved to the present moment. Something is giving itself away. Something is releasing itself into form. Something is outpouring itself, and as the great teacher said, "The rain falls on the just and the unjust," meaning those who can receive it, have it. Those who can't receive it, don't have it.

Receptivity is dependent upon the attitudes of mind. It is not dependent upon economic situations, although we try to tell ourselves that it is. It is dependent on one thing only, and that is your mental attitude. You are the only thinker in your mind, so you can determine what your mental attitude is to be. The Divine Givingness, this Prospering Mind, as I call It, is forever active whether you get into the stream of Its action or whether you stay out of it.

People will continue to make money for as long as you and I are alive. Many people will make lots of money. Others will go along struggling, straining, and groaning right to their death, because they do not realize that mental attitudes make the difference between riches and poverty. "To him that hath shall be given, and from him who hath not, even that which he hath shall be taken." This is a law of consciousness.

Therefore, it all begins and ends in the individual, not in the collective unit.

ENLARGE YOUR PATTERNS

When you think in terms of money, never think in terms of a definite sum. You may be limiting your potential. Never underestimate your worth. What is bound to happen if you do is illustrated by a general example in *The Science of Mind* textbook, and I feel that the gist of this message bears repeating here. However, I am going to upgrade the salaries of the four men concerned, because wages have risen considerably since this book was written.

Four men were involved. John received a salary of $75 a week. Bill's wages were $100 a week; Jim's were $125, and Charles earned $150. All of these men lost their jobs and each went to a New Thought practitioner for spiritual treatment in order to obtain another job. One would naturally assume that each wanted more money.

In cases similar to the ones we are talking about, the practitioner works with the thought that there is nothing but activity. He thereby heals the belief in inactivity and declares that the individual concerned is Divinely active, occupied, and compensated. Without question the practitioner sets a mental law in motion which will produce something for each of the individuals treated. His treatment is good and effective. If the individuals accept it as being so, each man finds a position. As a result, John receives $75 a week; Bill gets $100, Jim goes to work for $125, and Charles, once more, receives $150.

Why didn't each man receive a higher salary? Or why didn't all receive at least as much as Charles? The practitioner spoke the same words for each. But the law of mental equivalents, or imaging what you want, was at work. There was a lack of expectancy of greater good on the part of each of the men. Each wanted nothing more than his old salary again; none of them aspired to anything higher. Ernest Holmes' comment was this: "Each attracted unto himself, out of the Universal Good, that which he could comprehend—that which he believed he would get."

WHAT CAN YOU DO?

Beneficence is seeking to get into your mind and affairs. How are you going to let It in? First of all, you must think in Its terms. You can't think contrary to the Infinite Giver and expect to have Its gifts. In simple terms: You cannot doubt. You cannot think—even once—that what you desire probably won't come to you. This would be true of health. This would be true of any other form of experience you might desire. You have to think in Mind's terms of total possibility in order to have Its ideas function in your consciousness.

You have to retrain your subconscious mind so that your reactions regarding money are positive, so that you have no fear of having it or not having it. You know that the Divine Source is available to you at all times. You do not give money excess power, but see it for what it really is: a means of exchange, the means of freedom.

I am reminded here of one of the great English teachers of metaphysics, F. L. Rawson. He once told an audience that when he began his teaching he was in need of money. He decided he would treat fifteen minutes each day for one year, solely for money, ease, comfort, and prosperity. Within a few weeks his whole financial condition changed. He had no more concern about money, yet he maintained the treatments for a year, destroying the *lack* pattern in his subconscious mind. He replaced it with a prosperity pattern and was prosperous for the rest of his life.

Most people are conditioned to distrust other people's use of money. They are in awe of money. Yet they grumble because they don't have it. You can only demonstrate what you like. You can only demonstrate what you agree with. If you do not have prosperity now, think back to what your habitual attitudes on money are. This will explain a great deal. Then decide that money is good, that it is a Divine idea, and that you want to have it in your life. You can demonstrate money, as I have helped people do countless times in my consultation work.

AGAINST ALL MAN-MADE ODDS

The power and wisdom of Mind have never planned a negative program for anyone. This was true in the Depression years of the early thirties as it is today when we have a high percentage of unemployment and many job-seekers feel that the future is bleak for them.

For all of those who face discouragement, because they do not know a way out, I want to retell, in part, an experience that I related in greater detail in one of my earlier books, *The Science of Successful Living.**

Early in 1932, in the depths of the Depression, a woman came to me explaining that she was nearly destitute. She begged me to show her a way to change her consciousness so she could have prosperity and freedom in money.

"What is the one thing above all others that you would like to do?" I asked. She replied that she had always wanted to be a pastry specialist. At this point of economic crisis she couldn't even have found a job as a regular baker, let alone a specialist in fancy pastries.

She looked at me in complete amazement when I said, "Then go ahead and do it. If we together subconsciously accept the idea that you can be this, then every door will open for you to do it." She did not argue, but agreed. I gave her a mental treatment suitable to her problem, and asked her to use it daily.

We both believed her desire to be sound, even though the world would never have called it practical. In ways beyond anything the human mind would have thought

---

*Raymond C. Barker, *The Science of Successful Living* (1957; Marina del Rey, Calif.: DeVorss & Company, 1982).

possible, a noted manufacturer of flours arranged a one-week pastry school at the Waldorf-Astoria Hotel in New York City. Out of thousands of applicants, the woman who was following my counseling was one of those chosen. Upon completing the course she was considered so unusual that she was offered a job as a pastry specialist in one of the few wealthy clubs able to survive during the Depression. She was constantly employed in that type of work at the finest clubs and hotels for many years, receiving a large salary.

This was not a miracle. It depended on her belief that a larger mind than her own could cause the thing she desired to happen.

What any one person can do, you can do also in your own way. Creative Cause plays no favorites. Neither does the Infinite count blessings. Divine Mind doesn't count the wealth It bestows. It doesn't count the health, the love, the inspiration that is ever flowing out. It doesn't count the steps of progress you make, nor does it count those steps in nature. There isn't a person in the world who can give me the actual figure on how many leaves will fall in any of our national parks when the autumn season is here. That many, and more, will come out, fresh and green, in the spring.

The Infinite knows only to release. It knows only originality. It released you as originality by means of individuality, with the freedom to create attitudes which, in turn, determine the way of your life. Your invisible patterns of mind can always be enlarged.

YOUR CONDITIONED SUBCONSCIOUS

We have had thousands of years of belief that having money was sinful. We have, therefore, a strong conditioned pattern in the subconscious mind of the race. The group or universal subconscious mind has a memory pattern that money isn't really very nice. We have the vow of poverty in the monastic orders. Other people take similar vows. As a result there is a group subconscious resentment of people who have money.

That, perhaps, explains why so many people have an avid interest in how the other fellow spends his money. You may have caught yourself speculating on how John Jones could afford a new car, or how your friend Sally really was able to pay for a mink coat. Those are matters that are none of your concern.

Recently two students of our teaching were walking down a residential street in New York City. The gentleman said, "See, there's a sign in the window: *Three-room apartment for rent, $260.*" "Oh," his companion exclaimed, "I know a young man who is looking for an apartment, but he could never afford that price." A few moments later she looked guiltily at the man walking beside her and said apologetically, "I should never have said that, should I?" He smiled and said, "Well, I negated it in consciousness as soon as you said it."

The financial affairs of others are none of your business. You and I should not gossip about another's investments, be they good or bad in our own estimation. If a neighbor wants to go to the racetrack and lose a thousand dollars, it is no one's concern but his own. That doesn't mean that horseracing is bad; it doesn't mean that betting is bad. I am merely implying here that each individual has a right to make his own decision about his spending. If it is unwise, he will learn about it soon enough.

I recall an alert woman of sixty-eight who came to me with a disturbed mind. She had passed the company's regular age of retirement, but had used what is sometimes called a woman's prerogative and not reported her birth date accurately. So she continued to work, but because she no longer had faith in her true capabilities, she worked at a lesser job and a lesser salary. "When I was doing the work that I loved, and making a lot of money, I spent it freely, had good clothes, and a good time," she told me. "During those days I used to say laughingly, I'm going to be a poor old lady but I won't care then."

I was aghast at the pattern of limitation that she had planted in her subconscious mind. "Did you actually say and believe that?" I asked. She admitted that she had repeated that statement many times in what she believed to be jest. But her subconscious mind took her at her word, and she was fast using up her small salary and her savings. "I know now that I don't want to be poor," she told me. "I want to make more money."

We went to work on the woman's subconscious, negating her foolish statement that she would be a poor old lady, and planting the positive desire for continued work and prosperity. Today, three years later, this woman, independent of her company, has actively resumed a career in a creative field which she had almost cast aside. She knows that Divine Givingness is on her side. She believes, therefore she receives.

If you are one of those people who are frustrated because you haven't freedom of action, because you are limited in money, do something to overcome the frustration. It is keeping the unlimited supply from your door.

When you start to think prosperity and believe that money is spiritual, you will be clearing your frustration. However, you may have to undo a great deal of the past. You may have to lessen your remembrance of early years and early family patterns. Check yourself to see what erroneous money ideas may have developed in your consciousness. Then disengage yourself from them. Innumerable individuals who were born in very limited circumstances were *not* conditioned by them. They rose either to prominence or at least to a place of pleasant financial security.

It requires self-discipline to think of money as spiritual and to honestly believe that you can be a recipient of Divine beneficence if you follow certain guidelines. There is no simple formula. Wise men have always known that what you believe determines what you receive.

A remarkable example of this occurred not long ago. A woman whom I have known for several years came into my office with a problem which concerned her greatly.

"I want to go to Europe," she said, "but I don't have enough money." I suppose the average person would have said, "It's preposterous. You are asking the impossible."

I, however, believe in the possible, not in the impossible. "Let's talk about it," I said. We reviewed her numerous other trips to Europe and talked about how much she had enjoyed them. Together we visualized the streets she had walked, the points of interest that she had found most enchanting. Having visited Europe many times myself, we were on familiar ground when I said, "Now actually see yourself in those places; get the feeling that you are there. Know that it is possible for you to be there."

She followed my suggestion, silently imaging the scenes and the pleasures she had known. We followed this with a spiritual treatment, and the formerly disturbed individual left my office in a state of expectancy.

Two days later there was a call from this woman. "I received a wire from a friend in San Francisco," she reported. "My friend told me that she was going to Europe on a business trip and invited me to go along as her guest."

This was a Divine answer to a believer's desire and expectancy.

Not all prosperity comes so easily. People often come into my office and say, "I want a million dollars." I tell them that is fine, if they are willing to work for it. But it may mean getting to work at seven in the morning and going home at eleven at night for about ten years. It may mean working all day Saturday and half of Sunday. This could be nothing but drudgery, or it could lead to the desired prosperity. Remember, your prosperity depends on your mental attitude and your belief that there is a Divine Givingness, giving to all who are able to receive.

Far too many people have a poverty pattern in their subconscious, and a mental attitude of laxness and laziness. They want to work from nine to five and their earning potential probably is less than $10,000 a year. No person can prosper in a large amount who habitually gets to the office a few minutes after nine and has to leave at a quarter to five in order to avoid the rush. At the lunch hour there usually is a doctor's appointment or a dentist's appointment, or a hairdresser's appointment, or some urgent shopping. You don't get a million dollars that way. Yet there is nothing implausible in wanting that million if you are willing to work for it. You can streamline your thinking to the point where you want to go, and go there.

Your intellect will come in and argue. It will try to sell you down the river of defeat. Your friends will tell you that what you are trying to do is impossible. You can believe them and relax, and go nowhere. Why not be a profitable thinker? Discipline yourself to have a minimum of worry and a minimum of fear. Train your thinking to patterns of maximum expectancy. The profitable thinker is never lazy, indolent, or stupid. He is always an alert, vital, creative, forward-looking individual. He has to have a personal sense of responsibility for his own individual life.

Jesus, who was the eldest son, walked out on his family when, according to tradition, he should have stayed home and taken care of his mother. He walked out on a traditional pattern because he saw that the world needed a new idea, and he had that idea.

In a similar way, you walk out on some set traditional belief if you want to emerge with a new idea. This doesn't necessarily mean that you need to get away from your relatives. You need to get away from that which is not profitable.

The businessman, examining his accountant's statements, asks: "What's eating up the profits?" He searches for the answer and concentrates on ways and means of increasing profit and of decreasing any waste of profit.

You can do as the businessman does by watching your mind and cutting out unprofitable thinking. Ask yourself: "Where is the waste, not in my life but in my thinking?" Check the profit sheet of what your mind has produced in the last forty-eight hours. If you see nothing but waste there, stop it. Find your hidden assets and see where the point of concentration should be. It takes a bit of *alone* thinking to do it, and that applies to everyone whose desire is prosperity and whose expectancy is money or its equivalent.

CHAPTER

VII

LET NOTHING
DETER YOU

———

You are mind and emotion, created with a free will to experience good or evil. Your mind and emotions are invisible, but the good or bad results of your use of them are visible in your life.

Each of us exists in and is a part of a perpetual immediacy. We are never out of the Creative Process. We are never out of that which the world has called God. We are always in that wisdom, that love, that greatness, that potential, that which is forever creating that which shall be.

When we experience negatives it is because we have created them. Therefore, we need to use the power that is within us to remove from our lives everything that is not good or pleasant. That means we need to neutralize each negative as it becomes apparent. I happen to believe that evil is absolute nonsense. It is unnecessary. It is always temporary, unless you choose to hang onto it. Evil has no intelligence in it save the intelligence we give to it, yet in some way or other each of us is, now and then, tied down to it. How do we get our freedom?

First of all we must realize that evil is nothing but an action or reaction in the human mind. That is all it is. Where is unhappiness? It is in the mind and the emotions. Where is fear? It is in the mind and the emotions. Where is sorrow? It is in the mind and the emotions.

The mind and emotions are involved in thought, and in this teaching the only thing we are handling is thought. We are not manipulating any external force, because we do not believe in an external power. The route of spiritual evolution which we have chosen is a hard route. Handling thought is difficult and many people become discouraged. Then I sometimes suggest: "Why don't you take another route? Why don't you take the route of fasting? Why don't you go without something you want? Maybe that will make you better." It has never helped me, but we all know people who have sacrificed something in order to be spiritual, or people who may go into rigid disciplines. Many of these acts are deemed worthy, and it is possible that they have helped multitudes down through the ages.

NEGATIVES ARE NEVER PERMANENT

I know that the assault on the negatives of my world can be made by my mind and my mind only. If I am deterred in any way, it is because I have slipped into a side alley of belief in which I remain entrapped until I wake up and say I have had enough of this nonsense. Then I clear my consciousness and firmly cast out the negative that is acting as a roadblock to my spiritual progress.

A woman in San Francisco, who later became one of our famous teachers, had been a chronic invalid all her life. When she first went to hear one of our speakers, she listened and believed. Returning home she busied herself at what she felt she must do. Her husband came in and exclaimed, "What ever are you doing, my dear?" She was pouring all of her expensive medicines down the sink. "I've decided to get well," she said, and she did. There is nothing wrong with medicine, and we have a high respect for members of the medical profession. However, this woman had arrived at the conclusion that the problem was within herself. She had also arrived, either consciously or unconsciously, at the conclusion that the solution of her problem was within herself. She started to act upon it and got the desired result.

I could give innumerable instances where this has been done—where a person went along in the valley of the shadow of death and finally decided to come out in the light. Having decided in his or her own mind to leave the shadows and seek the light, the individual kept thinking on that high plateau where only the good could happen. Many refuse to believe in the permanency of evil. Negatives are never permanent. They only change form and seem to be.

Any negative in your life, or in my life, is a temporary negative and can be handled in the mind, provided we know how to do it. If we don't choose to handle it, we can accept it as an invited guest. We can nourish it with our attention, our weeping and wailing, and our gnashing of teeth. We can secure the pity of our loved ones, our neighbors, and our friends. We can be brave and we can be heroic, and later we will be remembered for the wonderful way in which we bore our trials and tribulations.

That is not what I want said of me when I go to the other side of life. I want to be praised because I solved a few problems. You want to be praised for the same reason. I am not interested in great fortitude on the negative side of life. I am interested in people who are creative, people who are doing something, people who are not letting negatives ensnare them.

You and I know people who are letting this happen; people who have begun to slumber and sleep in their problems instead of seeking a spiritual way of solving them. One of the most interesting statements of Paul in writing to a very alive, alert audience, is: "Awake thou that sleepest and arise from the dead." He said this because he saw them slumbering in their acceptance of negatives.

At the Garden of Gethsemane, when Jesus came out for the last time, he said to his disciples: "Sleep on now, and take your rest." Meaning for the disciples, you are caught up in the whole negative picture, you are embroiled in all the negatives of the situation. Go right on thinking that way, feeling that way, and reacting that way. I can't do anything more about it. Sleep on and take your rest.

Sometimes a negative is very comforting to an individual. It makes him or her feel quite important. If there is a negative in your subconscious, don't let it affect you like an anesthetic, causing all your sensitivities to slumber. Get rid of it. You and I have to watch our minds morning, noon, and night.

ERADICATE YOUR NEGATIVES

Anyone can be cheerful on a bright, sunny day, but what about the day when it is pouring rain? Do you look out of the window and say, "Oh, what a miserable day?" Then immediately go into a deep depression?

There are plenty of negatives lurking about, infecting this individual and that. Guilt, fear, doubt, and anxiety are common examples. Many people suffer from a pattern of lack in their subconscious minds, as was pointed out when we discussed prosperity. Hate, envy, jealousy, avarice, and anger all can be added to the list. One or more of which needs to be eradicated from your mind. What about loneliness and unhappiness? You do not want them. Then there is resentment, which, if harbored within, can ruin your whole life—not the life of the person you resent.

One of my friends told me that she had read my book *The Science of Successful Living* many times, but she always had skipped over the chapter entitled "Resentment Is Ruin" because she couldn't think of anyone or anything that she resented. Then one morning she decided to read the chapter. The first three sentencs caused her to pause and take another look at herself. They are: "Resentment is an abnormal direction of the emotion with an unconscious intent of self-destruction. Its indulgence creates havoc in every area of your life. It is harmful to the body, your business, your friendships, and your finances."

Those words caused the reader to look at herself squarely. It took only a few minutes for her to find several resentments, both of people and of situations. She soon realized that she had been skipping the chapter because subconsciously she was afraid of what she would find out about herself. Consciously she had convinced herself she didn't have a resentment in the world.

When it comes to your own negatives, you many need to do a little searching to find them. Many people would deny that they have any of the emotional patterns that we call negatives, but there are few of us who are blameless in that direction. When you find a negative, don't harbor it. Clear your consciousness as quickly as possible, and note the reawakening of your real self, emotionally and mentally.

GOOD IS NORMAL

It often is difficult to get people to believe that any form of good is normal and natural, and that they should have it. If you don't have an abundance of good in your life, it is because you never created it out of yourself. You have wanted someone else to create it for you. You have expected it to come from some external change. However, if an external change brings you good, it is because you have created the external change.

As without, so within. As within, so without. This great hermetic axiom of many thousands of years ago remains true today. We accept it as meaning that the inside and the outside are two facets of one state of consciousness. The without and the within are one, and that's why every false facade begins to crack after a while.

When I know that the universe around me and the universe within me are one universe, one process, one idea, and when I know my interior universe is in the same mathematical order as is the external cosmos, then I'll project the good that I want. However, I have to put the inside in order, if I intend to have order on the outside. If the stars in their courses, and the planets, and suns, and moons were as disorderly as most people's thinking, we wouldn't be here. If this great cosmic system in which we are functioning were as disorderly as the many men and women who are going through each day worried, doubting, fearful, and feeling guilty, there would be nothing but chaos.

When you get the feeling that everything is wrong, and you want to blame the world instead of yourself, stand in front of the mirror for a few minutes. Then laugh. There is healing power in looking at yourself in the mirror and laughing at yourself. Perhaps when a monkey laughs at himself when he sees his face in a mirror, he is smarter than we are.

It is interesting that no animal has ever had a chronic disease until it was domesticated. No animal has ever been overweight until it was domesticated. There seems to be a special animal know-how, when animals are in their natural state, that keeps them in tune with their own good and their own environment.

You and I, who are thinkers, whereas the animals are not, may sometimes know too much for our own good. There is one certainty, however, that we must always be conscious of. We exist in and are a part of something that responds to us. This is something that the world does not know. People are weary of the old concepts of God. They are weary of the old theology. They are weary of the stained-glass windows. Yet they cannot see that there is an immediacy in which they are forever immersed and in which they are forever a part. It can be experienced. It can be explored. It can be known, and it is good.

CLEAR YOUR THINKING

We must clear our thinking on evil. It is neither person, place, nor thing. It is an action and a reaction in the human mind. Because it is this action and reaction of mind, of thought and feeling, man can control it. He may not, but he can.

When you experience a temporary evil, you must locate the point where it is. Many individuals try to locate this evil in someone else. They locate it in situations, in conditions, or in this way or that. They are wrong. The sole existence of evil is in consciousness.

We are not the first people to say this. It has been said by many wise men and women for as far back as there is any record of philosophy or religion. Jesus said, speaking of the devil, "Get thee behind me Satan" and "For he is a liar and the father of it." Those are very good statements. Whatever negative force seemingly is operating upon a situation, group, or individual is a lie. Being a lie, it can be cleared, because there is always the truth to clear every lie. There is always that which will clarify. Know the opposite of the negative that is bothering you and affirm that opposite. State the positive in consciousness—not weakly or wistfully, but definitely. Say: *This shall not control me. This shall not operate me. This shall not confound me. I stand at a point of control. I stand at a point of poise. I use my mind as it was intended to be used, for a creative, intelligent projection of life.*

When someone says, "Yes, that's a beautiful philosophy," you know that person is not going to use it. Most people, when they are all caught up in negatives, don't want creative thinking. They don't want to be told how to get out of their troubles. They want consolation, sympathy, and someone on the outside to help them get out. I'm not saying people should not help one another at the material level. I'm saying that you and I have to clarify our own consciousness.

LIFE IS AN INSIDE THING

I have to handle my negatives myself. I have to make whatever changes are necessary *in myself*, so that I can function as a creative person. If I allow the negatives of life to deter me, to hold me back, to deprive me of my victory over life, then I am my own worst enemy. I can't blame it on anyone else.

In the case of one individual a psychotherapist may discover the emotional cause behind the problem. Strangely, however, another individual may have the same emotions and no problem. You and I were given dominion over our world. The Bible says that God gave man dominion. Let's add another interesting statement: " . . . Strait is the gate and narrow is the way, which leadeth unto life, and few there be that find it." We find truth in this statement because there are only a few—meaning certain people—who can see life as the action of consciousness instead of nothing but a material operation to be manipulated by material ways and means.

Life is an inside thing. It is not merely the circulatory

system of your body, or the ordered functioning of your heart. It is the action of consciousness. Why are there few that find it? Because the others don't want to use an interior method to get what they want. They want to use external methods. They push, shove, and grab. They use every method, ethical and unethical, moral and immoral, to get where they want to go. When they get there they are a little tired, but they are very proud. It is sad to know that inside these people there is a sickness; whether they know it or not there is a terrific dissatisfaction.

In contrast, there are many people achieving their goals who are not deterred by any evil, and who arrive at the place they want to go by straight, clear, right thinking, right motivation, right direction, and right desires. This doesn't mean withdrawal from the world. It doesn't mean a false piety and it doesn't mean a system of salvation. It merely means that the person is honest with himself or herself, and with his fellowmen; that he or she is going right ahead on an honest program which is one of integrity. The person is going ahead on a program of basic goodness. It can be done. You and I can do it.

STOP FIGHTING YOURSELF

We have been trained to fight in the external world, not realizing that the real fight is in our internal world. The inside fight is the fight against yourself. I remember that some years ago I read Karl Menninger's great book *Man Against Himself.* It made a strong impression on me because he was saying, as a psychiatrist, that you and I are fighting ourselves.

When you fight yourself you are in serious trouble. I remember a gentleman of our church who came to me several years ago. He had been undergoing psychiatric treatment for years, and going from one psychiatrist to another, which, of course, was wrong. When he came to me, and I am not a psychiatrist, he said, "They tell me that my own inner anger is destroying me."

As I listened I noted the ire underneath and tried to show him how to handle it. He was a very kindly gentleman on the outside. He was neither gruff nor rude. He was successful and much beloved. He had built a facade which had not yet begun to crack, and the trouble was all on the inside. I tried to give him guidelines for conquering his anger, but each time I believed I was helping him he went off to another doctor. Why did he do this? He wanted reconfirmation that the problem was not his fault. At no time was I able to calm him enough to let it sink into his mind that the only thing he was fighting was himself. Intellectually he knew it, but I couldn't get him to do the inside work which had to be done to get rid of his anger.

In early times the superstitious and the primitive used the idea of devils to explain their problems, and the tradition was carried on in early religions. There are millions of people today who believe in a literal devil.

There is no devil. We are consciousness, and we can handle that. We are specialists in knowing that clarified, correct thinking, in an arena of balanced emotions, can correct any negative situation. You don't get this by listening, listening, listening, and reading, reading, reading. There has to come the time when you put the book down and look into the mirror. You say, "Now I see it. Now I see that my consciousness has been wrong." You can say it without guilt and without blame. Then you consciously dedicate yourself to thinking and feeling what you want. When you do this you are set free.

RULES FOR EFFECTIVE LIVING

No matter where we are, what our age level is, or what our financial or social level may be, all of us want better living. We should have it and can have it. Again, the important thing is to get rid of destructive negatives. Several years ago Manly Palmer Hall, one of the greatest of the living philosophers, wrote a booklet entitled *Ten Basic Rules for Living.* In it he said that one of the first laws of ancient wisdom was *Stop Worrying.* He said that you can find this in the most ancient records of Egypt, India, and China. The Judeo-Christian tradition also is one of *Don't Worry.*

Some of the most magnificent statements in the Old Testament are *Non-Worry* statements, such as "Be not afraid for I, the Lord, thy God am with thee withersoever thou goest." That wisdom is some 3,500 years old.

Why did the ancient teachers, ancient philosophers, and founders of religion sense this wisdom? It was because they beheld the people in their own day mortgaging their futures. Take the man who lived almost in serfdom on a little plot of ground, with no comforts according to our standards, no real reason for living, because there was no money to make and no future. Yet the teachers and philosophers observed that he mortgaged his future, whatever it might be, every time he worried.

I was much interested in these facts because I have always assumed that the "Don't Worry" advice was fairly modern—let us say, perhaps since the Renaissance. But is seems that wise men always have counseled: Be not afraid.

You may say, "Counseling is well and good, but will it work?" Once again I say, "Stand in front of your mirror and say in a determined voice: *I am not afraid, for the power of life is the power of my soul, and I am not afraid.*"

Another rule that Mr. Hall stressed is that we should stop forever trying to possess people. We try to mold others in our own image. We say, "Do it because it is good for you" or "It will improve your looks, or your chances to make more friends."

You are mortgaging your future when you try to mind someone else's business, because you are not letting yourself be yourself. The Bible says that you should give yourself away, but that doesn't mean that you are to be opinionated and bossy. It means communication with others and the giving of a free field of ideas—a free field of emotion. You are really harming yourself when you try to arrange someone else's life.

Another important rule, which I have often stressed, is *Learn to Relax.* Every religion that has ever appeared on the face of the globe has given its followers some means of being quiet. Only in a moment of stillness can you relax, and only when you are relaxed do you see things as they are. This idea probably explains the therapeutic value of the Twenty-third Psalm. I am sure it has relaxed more people than any other single piece of scripture. Take the single sentence: *The Lord is my shepherd, I shall not want.* I have seen people heal their bodies with that statement. They merely said: "I shall not want health. It is mine."

I talk to somewhere between fifteen and twenty people a week, who come to my office with problems. Inevitably they leave me saying they feel better. Now, I am not fooled by the idea that I have any special power. I don't. But I think they feel relaxed because they are seated in a fairly comfortable chair and in a handsome room where there is no radio and no television. There is no newspaper and there is no one else around. For thirty minutes they forget about subways and taxis. They forget the work to be done and the pressures. They have conversed quietly and thoughtfully. Usually the time we spend together is concluded with a spiritual treatment.

No matter that when the individual is back on the street all the little annoyances crop up and the individual is back in the modern tempo of life. No matter. There is nothing wrong with that for any of us, if we have our moments of pause.

Another point Mr. Hall stressed is our need to accumulate. He cites the ancient wisdom which is the *Law of Nonpossession.* He reminds us that none of the great spiritual teachers accumulated possessions. They never hung onto things. They never retained, but almost all of them gave everything away.

In a modern economy you can't give everything away, but a basic rule is don't overaccumulate. Have the freedom to walk through life without too many strings holding you back. Have the freedom to move ahead, and walk with flexibility in the present. Philosophically, religiously, and psychologically *now* is the only instant there is.

Divine Mind moves forward without the impediment of a false concept of the need of things. Creative Cause uses things but is never in bondage to them. Live in the present with ease, but not with bondage. Your future is the present extended in time, and you can become what you know yourself to be.

CHAPTER

VIII

WHY, WHAT, AND
WHERE ARE YOU?

—

You are invisible. No one has ever seen you, because you are consciousness.

A number of years ago, Emma Curtis Hopkins, a teacher in this field of thought, said the greatest statements ever made were: *Look unto me and be ye lifted up* and *The greatest thing a man can do is turn to Infinite Mind.* Isaiah said: "Look unto me, and be ye saved, all the ends of the earth: for I *am* God, and *there is* none other."

Define it as you will, there is a God. There is a Wisdom, an Intelligence, a Life, a Love, a Power, a Creative Process. Call it what you will, there is something that causes things to happen.

Belief is the law of life. We stand in a Divine Givingness which responds to us as we give it a pattern to which it can respond. We have to take the cup to the faucet to fill it. When we know what we want, life can give it to us.

The metaphysicians have always said that man was an idea in the Mind of the Universe. And in their theories they have always said that creation and the process that is forever creating is that of mind, idea and expression. The only form of life by which an Infinite Knower, an Infinite Thinker, can release ideas and have them expressed is by means of man. That, no doubt, is the reason for our evolution. We evolved under a plan and pattern, in an order, because it was the only way in which the creative principle, Mind, could express Its ideas. "All evolution is evidence of a progressive Mind thinking in new terms to bring forth improvement. This process is in you; in fact it is what you are."*

You are the Infinite Mind reduced to visibility (body) proclaiming Its ideas by means of your consciousness. But you as consciousness are invisible. No one can see that inner you that thinks and feels and expands into ever greater knowingness, but the effects of the operative forces generated by your consciousness are clearly visible in your life. You are a thinker, whether you want to be or not. Things happen because you think and let your feelings guide you. If your thoughts and desires are positive and filled with an expectancy that some specific good will happen, and if you think and expect it consistently as you plant the idea in your subconscious mind, the good will happen.

If your thoughts and emotions are consistently negative and your "common sense" tells you: "You are expecting too much"; "It might happen to John Jones but it will never happen to you"; or "You can't, because you don't know how," then you will, through the law of cause and effect,

*Raymond C. Barker, *The Power of Decision* (New York: Putnam Publishing Group, 1968), P.62.

experience failure and disappointment. The seed of negation is as easily planted in the subconscious as is the positive seed. In this way, by thinking and expecting, either
positively or negatively, you control the events of your
life.

You are more than just a getting, giving individual.
There is more to life than just paying bills, and doing
good works. That *something more* is what I call individuality; it is the Infinite Intelligence in you at the very center of your being. Individuality includes intuition, which
is not a matter of hunches that you play at the racetrack,
but a matter of self-awareness. When you know yourself
as *I am consciousness*, new ideas, new perceptions enter
your thinking. Individuality also includes what we have
called the spirit in man, which is inexplicable, yet know-
able in part.

If you and I are more than name and number, more
than background, environment and culture, more than
education, more than experience, then this thinking-feel-
ing mind, an individualization of the Divine Mind, is what
we are, and that is what operates our lives day after day,
throughout a lifetime and throughout eternity.

THE AGE-OLD QUESTION, "WHY WAS I BORN?"

Philosophically and spiritually there is one primary answer: The universe cannot be a matter of chance. A Creative Mind could only fully express itself by creating a self-
conscious being. You are a self-conscious being. I am a
self-conscious being. Every individual who is born, bar-
ring none, is created a self-conscious being, and each indi-

vidual is unique. That means that no one ever created, in the past, present, or future, is like another human being. No matter how much you may love and admire someone, you cannot be like that person. The pattern is Divine, and in its uniqueness it is created but once. No two patterns are created according to the same mold, and no two are created for the same purpose.

That places a tremendous responsibility on each of us, if we only realize it, but it also endows each one of us with great freedom of choice; freedom of self-determination. No one else was created to accomplish exactly what you were created to achieve. But, remember, you do not have to do it alone. "The Father in me, he doeth the work." The father in you, your subconscious, is the doer, acting upon the thoughts and emotions of your conscious mind.

Most people don't ask the question "Why was I born?" unless they are in trouble. If things are going well they may instinctively know that they were born to inherit their rights of birth: health, prosperity, happiness, and self-expression. Others may not know this at all. They may believe they were born to struggle and strain and suffer. They are the ones who blame the world, their neighbors, their relatives, the stock market, the President, or just hard luck for the difficult situations they find themselves in.

Because none of us is perfect—though we strive for perfection—somewhere along the way in every life there is likely to come the question "Why was I born?"

You were born to be an integral part of the progression of life. As I have said before, the evolution of mankind cannot be a matter of chance. People say to me, "I do not believe in God, but I believe in evolution." So I say,

"Who planned evolution? What was the intelligence that planned evolution?" As we see it, there is an Eternal Intelligence of Mind, unfolding out of Itself an intelligent system by means of which to express Itself. That's evolution. Evolution is the result of an Intelligent Thinker thinking intelligently according to a plan, a process, a way by which It can express Itself.

YOU ARE A DIVINE NECESSITY

We are the only level of life which knows itself. The dog does not know it is a dog. The cow does not know it is a cow. The horse does not know it is a horse. These animals may be trained to respond to a name, and often to many commands, but they do not know they are animals, or what kind of animals they are. They only know how to be what they are. You, in contrast, exist because the Infinite *must have you* in order to be aware of Itself. You are a Divine necessity.

You are the instrument through which Creative Mind gets things done. For instance, Thomas Edison was the instrument through which First Cause gave to the world a knowledge of electricity and how to use it. The Wright Brothers' ideas of the possibility of flight in the air were Divine ideas passed on to mankind through the thinking and emotions—and the belief—of Orville Wright and his brother. Every invention, every scientific or medical discovery and every advance in the industrial world, the financial world, the world of arts and crafts, and every other sphere of accomplishment, is the achievement of the Infinite Mind working through the individual self-conscious mind. Sometimes many individuals contribute to a project, but each individual use of mind has its own specific function. Our manned flights to the moon are examples of this. So are the operations of great hospitals or great industrial plants. Every activity throughout the world involves God operating through man. When results seem evil instead of good, it is evidence of some misguided use of the Power within.

You are as necessary to life as life is necessary to you. You are not an infinitesimal being wandering around in a universe, lost in the miasma, the fog, of doubt and fear. You are a living soul. You are the image and likeness of your Creator. You are the glory of Life.

WHY HAVEN'T YOU HEARD THIS BEFORE?

Many of you have heard it and believed it. Many have not, and for many reasons. It was not until the last several generations that this could be said without fear of being condemned by the old churches. Jesus said it. Isaiah said it. Paul inferred it but he couldn't do anything about it. He was a theologian and theologians are so interested in working out theory that they forget practice. Jesus would never have remained in chains for years as Paul did.

CAN WE DEFINE THE CREATIVE MIND?

You are because *something* caused you to be. We, in the New Thought Movement, have called It by many names, but we do not believe in a Man-God in the sky. When you arrive at true spiritual understanding, you admit the na-

ture of a Creative Power and you don't try to understand
it totally. You understand as much as you can. Any person
who says he can define God completely is wrong. Any religious doctrine that has a total answer to what God is,
and what man is in his entirety, is wrong. These are unanswerable questions, but they are questions into which
we can do a great deal of fathoming. You can launch out
and receive greatly through your search.

Once again—*Why am I?* Because something caused me
to be and humanity was the means by which God could
become Divinity. Humanity is the means by which an
Infinite Mind can discover Itself.

WHAT ARE YOU?

*The what you are is what you have done with the why
you are.* That may sound complicated but it isn't. During
the first eight years of your life you have had very little to
say about what took place. Everything was determined
for you. You were totally preconditioned by the place you
lived in, the relatives, the family, the immediate emotional
life, particularly your mother's and father's reaction to
you. From the age of eight to about twenty most people
just accepted what they were told. Today, however, even
teen-agers are asserting themselves and sometimes revolt-
ing against dictates or advice of their elders. But generally,
at least a few years ago, the process of growing up involved such ideas as *go ahead and do what others do,* or
fight it, resist it, quarrel with it. By and large, the thinking
was go ahead in some way and give little thought to it.

I was born into a family whose name was Barker. They

were a definite type. My background, way back on my father's side, was from one country, and way back on my mother's side it was from another. We lived in a comfortable home, ate wholesome food, and led a more or less average social life. Just like most of the rest of you, I made no attempt to change the first eight years of my life.

When you reached the age of rebellion, be it seventeen or thirty, you probably didn't have an intelligent plan. Rebellion, in itself, never produces intelligence. Rebellion only produces more rebellion. It is only when a situation has calmed down that you begin to see things in a sensible light—begin to evolve a workable plan for what you are going to do with your life. I'm presenting the hopeful picture. Many people go on and on and never ask the question. They are reasonably contented or, let me say, complacently adjusted to a nothingness of the spirit even though they may or may not have material wealth. Something is missing in their lives, and occasionally they wonder why life isn't the glorious experience of their expectation; occasionally they don't even know that it isn't.

The rebellion I spoke of earlier is like an explosive. It sets something in motion, but it doesn't solve a thing. Looking back in history, the thirteen original American colonies, when they were fighting England, were in rebellion. They talked about liberty and they went out and shot people for liberty, and they themselves were shot for liberty. It took another ten years before they discovered what they had done. Then after the rebellion was over, the ideal—which has become the United States of America—began to take shape.

So maybe you have rebelled. Maybe I did. But it was

only later that we began to say, "Wait a minute. I don't need to be like this." Then, as the Bible would say, *there comes healing with wings.* The moment an individual awakens to the fact that he or she does not need to be the way he is, that individual is started on the pathway of revelation—of self-awareness and self-realization.

Perhaps some members of your family, or other people you know, have totally accepted themselves as they are and do not believe they can change; they have no desire to change. So they are putting up with half a loaf instead of grasping the whole. *What they are is not responding to the why they are.*

The what you are is what you believe about yourself. The why you are is what the Infinite is eternally knowing you as being. Whenever we get a genius, a savior, or a saint, we get the man or woman who at the *what level* knows the *why level.* The genius of our great teachers is that they know that the self-expression of Divine Cause is the why of them and they decide that is what they are going to be instead of being the son or daughter of James and Mary Smith. Then they awaken to the fact that the two are not opposite. The two are one.

But as long as there is a belief in duality such as, "I am born to express life, but I really don't have a chance because there always has been a tendency toward bronchitis and asthma in our family. I just don't fight it any more. I go to the mountains in the summer, and if I can, I go to Tucson, Arizona, in the winter. In between I stop off in New York, where I have a little apartment. I wish I could live there all the time."

People who have chronic ailments, chronic financial

crises, worries, and frustrations don't get very far in being what they want to be or expressing the why of their existence. Then along comes a spiritual mind, an individual who says, "If I am the self-expression of Creative Mind, then I am not asthma, bronchitis, or a creature constantly affected by damp weather, hot air, dry weather, snowy weather, or any kind of climate. I am what I am whether I am under a palm tree or whether I'm walking in a park with three feet of snow."

When you have come to that awakening—that you can be what you want to be—then you know the real meaning of existence. But most people don't believe that. They want to believe that the universe is against them. That there is a plot somewhere aimed directly and specifically at them. You are what you have made yourself to be, or what you have accepted yourself as being, and what you believe about yourself conditions the center of you which is the why.

WHERE ARE YOU?

You are where you belong by right of your own thought. Your place in life right now is determined by your beliefs, your attitudes, your emotions, your concepts, your desires, or your lack of them. If you are not happy where you are, remember that where you are can always be changed. There is no person sitting in judgment. There is no condemnation. There is no last day of judgment, and no one is writing down in a little book all of your mistakes. The Infinite is not that interested. When you awaken to that belief, you are free of a great deal of delusion.

You can change the what you are and the where you are. The only thing you cannot change is the why you are. That remains unchangeable throughout eternity. All you have to do is move over on the affirmative side of life. Decide what you want, think what you want, act as though it were so, and it becomes so.

This is all that Jesus did. Jesus announced himself as he knew himself to be and proceeded to act as though it were so and it was so. "Well," you protest, "I'm not Jesus." Of course you are not. You are not supposed to be. You are supposed to be you. Don't be bothered with what you don't have. Work sincerely with what you have, and watch your progress in your spiritual well-being and in your material world as well.

If you have a worried mind, stop worrying. It won't be easy but you can do it gradually. Take five minutes out of your busy day, relax, and think of something pleasant, or something amusing. Then go back to your worries if you must. But make your pleasant relaxing period longer the next day. You can always reach out and grasp those worries to your bosom again if you want to, but if you practice nonworry and turn your attention to productive thinking, you'll find that you've taken one step toward changing the where you are.

DO YOU REALLY WANT TO CHANGE?

It all comes back to the question "Do you really want to change?" Because the why of you will give you what you want, if the what of you will change. Creative Mind at the center can only work through what you have put at the circumference.

The great danger in life is settling down. It was Emerson who said that it is only through the unsettled that great ideas can be born. One of the big difficulties with most of us is that our goals are short-termed. When you ask a person if he hasn't a long-range goal he shies away from it. If you ask, "What are you going to be three hundred years from now?" the answer is, "Oh, don't be silly." But you are going to be somewhere three hundred years from now and you are going to be something. Isn't it about time that you made up your mind?

Many people merely want to live long enough to get their pensions. Then they settle down in a dull routine along with a lot of other people who are collecting their pensions.

But when you think of yourself as a timeless, spaceless continuum that always has been, is now, and ever more shall be, your viewpoint is bound to change. Take time to perceive yourself as what you have conceived yourself to be. You are a frail human only because you have believed that you are a frail human and everyone has confirmed it to you.

When you believe that you can change yourself, not that somebody else can change you, you can do it. It is this great quality of consciousness, the ability to accept self-change, that is the hope of the world. So the limited can say they are free. The sick can say they are well. The unhappy can say they are glad, and the disturbed can say they are at peace. They can do this when they decide to switch from one side of the ledger to the other; when they decide that *why they are* and *what they are* are the same thing—self-expression.

There is no power of opposition. There is no condemnation. There is no evil to fight, and there is no hell toward which you can go. There is life to be lived. There is love to be loved. There is good to be aware of, and there is good to be given and received. There is a flow, a continuum, an expansion, and a greatness.

Only those who can grasp it can have it, because others are too busy thinking: Poor little me, I am unhappy, I am misunderstood, and nobody loves me. I am misinterpreted. Everyone else at the office gets ahead and I don't. So they sit in their own negation and disintegrate.

Then someone comes along who says, "There are no favorites in the kingdom of God. Every person is equal in the Divine order of things. I know that within me, as me, is a power that becomes what I decide I shall become. So now I cast off that which I do not want, and I see myself as that which I really am—what I want to be. I shall accept that which I do want because I am an unconditioned individual, except as I have conditioned myself. I am a free soul, save as I have put myself in prison. Now I unlock the doors that I used to shut, thinking they were a protection. Now I look out windows by raising the shades that I pulled down because I did not want to see. Now I behold what I really am because I have let in the light. I am a triumphant spiritual soul."

POSSIBILITY AND PROBABILITY

You no doubt have listened to many people who say this about almost any situation, "Yes, it is possible, but it isn't probable." There is a dual law of possibility and probability and your belief in one or the other has a great deal to do with the *what* and the *where* you are. We, in our science, deal with possibility and try to disregard probability. If you consult your Bible, you will find many references to possibility, but none to probability. Take this one, for instance. Jesus spoke to the father of a child who was troubled by a dumb spirit which often possessed the child and caused him to harm himself. The father sought Jesus' help. "He said unto him, 'If thou canst believe, all things are possible to him that believeth.' And the father of the child cried out, and said with tears, 'Lord, I believe; help thou mine unbelief.' "

As the story continues, we learn that the child was healed.

I believe that possibility is of the spirit and probability is of the human mind. Most people are limited by their belief in probability and their failure to hold fast to possibility. We say, here in the United States, that any child born in this country has the possibility of becoming the President of the United States. Then instantly we say that under the law of probability this little boy or (today) this little girl probably will not be President. With that we sign everything away. We tell young people that it is possible for any person to accomplish almost anything, but that they probably will fall into the routine of a set job and go no farther than that.

But let's turn back to possibility. Possibility denies everything from illness to old age, and all the other limitations you can think of. Stay at the point of possibility. Perhaps the genius of a mind like Jesus' was that he stayed at the point of possibility. He did not work with the law of probability. Perhaps this is why he could do the phenomenal things that he did. It was not probable that he should do them, but he didn't know that.

This week, why don't you and I go back to possibility? What can you be? Why aren't you?

In the Bible it states that "with God all things are possible," because the Divine Wisdom doesn't know what can't be done. The Divine Wisdom doesn't know you as a limited factor. It only knows you as a possibility. The Infinite Spirit doesn't know that you have self-conditioned yourself, unknowingly, but nevertheless you have self-conditioned yourself to the level of probability.

It is totally possible that you won't have a cold this year. It is totally possible that you won't get any touch of virus for the rest of your life. It is totally possible that you will get a better job, better home, or a better group of friends, or a better this or a better that. It is totally possible.

But when the human-mind wheels start going, the chances are that the answer will be, "Yes it is possible, but is it probable?"

The moment you deal with probability you sign away your birthright. With God all things are possible and you are a part of God. As I think back I realize that this entire instruction in the New Thought Movement arose and flourished, and is meeting the needs of millions of people, because enough of us stayed at the point of possibility and didn't go into the level of probability. Otherwise all the earlier teachers would have given up. All the early writers would never have written their books, and all the early healers would never have healed their people, if they hadn't stayed at the point of possibility.

In your own life say, "It can be done," and stay at that point long enough to see it done. Go back to something that has bothered you this past week, or the past days, or the past month, and stop thinking probability. Start knowing possibility.

INDIVIDUALITY, THE ESSENCE OF LIFE

The great philosophers have always talked about the individual being on his eternal search for Reality. I think I can say that in a simpler way: That is why you and I are never quite satisfied. There is an inner hunger and an inner thirst which is never fully met. So we, too, are on this pathway, this search, not necessarily to know our fellow men, but to know ourselves.

Prior to Sigmund Freud and his immediate followers, and their researches into the operation of the human mind, we had only religious concepts of man. We had man being manipulated by an external force. Later, men came along and gave us a new vision of man as the creative thinker and feeler, not merely a puppet on the end of a string. It was discovered that the mind in the individual is capable of self-healing. It also is capable of giving itself new directions.

The Creative Process is never stale, It is never bored, and It never repeats Itself. Watch your own thinking.

Look out for inner stagnation. Do you suffer from inner boredom, no longer seeking the new idea, the new concept? Do you go through an endless routine of living?

If the answer is yes, hasten to change, for stagnation, boredom, and routine are the three major destructive factors of illumined consciousness.

The wise have always said that in this universe there are no finalities. Nothing is ever totally complete. Everything is under a law of growth, and the essence of individuality is that law of growth. It is being unfolded. It is consciousness knowing itself in an infinite variety of ways. It is you. It is myself. You and I are on this search for the new, and we are up against only one thing: our own belief in limitation.

CHAPTER

IX

QUESTIONS HAVE ANSWERS

—

What you are looking at, you are seeing with your mind. What you are hearing, you are hearing with your mind. Your five senses deliver facts to the inner you. Sometimes these seeming facts are fiction, and you, inside your own mind, must determine what is the truth. This inner mind action is invisible. It is only your outward behavior that people can observe.

The mind that answers questions correctly progresses. The mind that is certain of itself is the creative mind. It is amazing to discover how few people are certain of their own minds. Far too many are living in doubt, questioning their abilities, questioning their own uncertainties. If we want New Thought ideas to be operative in our lives, we must be certain, definite, and creative.

We state our belief in this way: There is one Creative Mind in the universe. This Creative Mind is in all, through all, as all. You and I are the means by which It functions on this plane of life. When we make certain of each step that we take, we are truly expressing the spirit of Life. At times we must ask ourselves several questions in order to be sure we are making right decisions. Our minds should not accept all the ideas that come to us, without first analyzing them.

There are many individuals who say, "I know this is so because I read it in the newspaper." Others believe everything they read in books or hear in a television newscast. However, if you want to be free, do some thinking before you are certain. Ask some *whys*.

The world expects you to believe its ideas, and you often are considered peculiar if you don't. There is a lovely phrase in the writings of Peter where he says: "But ye are a chosen generation; a peculiar people." I like that phrase. When people say that we, of this instruction, are peculiar, I think that is one of the greatest compliments they can give us. It means we are forward-looking people who do not accept universal or traditional ideas and concepts without questioning. When anything appears to be doubtful, we ask why, and we do not cease asking until we have a satisfactory answer.

ALL KNOWLEDGE BEGAN WITH WHY?

We have no actual records of what early cavemen did, with the exception of some crude drawings on the walls of caves. These indicate a primitive intelligence. Therefore, it seems likely that the caveman asked, at least in his own mind, a great many questions about himself and his environment. Among them might have been these: "Why does the sun appear in the morning?" "Why does it disappear at night?" He undoubtedly wondered about the moon, too. Perhaps he asked, "Why do the leaves fall off the trees at a certain time and come back at another time?"

Gradually, it is supposed, the caveman began to answer some of his own questions, and this was the beginning of knowledge. Right here some traditionalist may ask, "Aren't you forgetting about Adam and Eve and the forbidden fruit?" That, of course, is an allegorical but not a factual portion of Biblical history. All knowledge, past and present, starts with the question, "Why?" The more you ask intelligent questions, the more alert, vital, and free you are.

Every life experience, be it good or bad, takes place for a reason, but not all people seek reasons. This was brought home to a young woman who had applied for an editor's job on a leading magazine. She knew her qualifications were excellent, and after an interview she truly expected to get the job. However, she did not, and she began to question her own capabilities. She became dejected; seriously concerned about the future of her career. Then she determined to swallow her pride and ask the agent who had sent her on the interview why she had been rejected. He told her that her qualifications were excellent, and had it not been for internal politics within the organization, she undoubtedly would have been given the job. Instead it was handed to a personal friend of one of the company officials. The young woman's self-respect was restored and she no longer feared for her future, all because she had the courage to ask why.

While giving a lecture on the West Coast recently, I stated that when you stop asking questions you are beginning to be senile. I don't know how well the listeners liked that, but I repeat, when you stop asking questions you have arrived at a point of mental deterioration.

THE TWO OLDEST QUESTIONS

Perhaps the two oldest questions in the world are: "Why was I born? and "Why must I die?" As a result of these two, early man probably originated some form of religion. Later religions, and all philosophical thought, came out of these two basic queries. People still ponder their answers, especially when depression takes over the working of the mind. These questions have never been answered fully, although I did cover our belief concerning the first one in some detail in an earlier chapter.

All religious systems have, in some way, tried to say to the individual: "This is why you were born, and this is why you die." Their opinions, their beliefs, their creeds have been as varied as the many ethnic groups out of which they came. In a number of instances religious doctrines have been definite and authoritative. We are not an authoritative spiritual teaching. We do not say a thing is so, and always will be so, because it always has been. We leave the individual free.

Among the concepts about life after death, there were various ideas of reincarnation, a future existence in heaven or hell, or total extinction. These ideas came along just as did the ideas that you and I were born because of a biological accident; or the idea that we were born because a deity somewhere needed us to experience sin and then later be cleansed. The traditionalists say that you and

I were born in sin, conceived in iniquity, and all the rest. There is not a word of truth in it, but it is a good theory for the people who want it.

In our philosophy we know that sin had nothing to do with it. I remember a great teacher of New Thought who said to me many years ago: "You were born at the right time, in the right place, by means of the right parents, in order to have a right experience." She said: "The Divine Intelligence never makes a mistake and you are not a mistake." I have never really wanted to live in another era, and I am happy to be right here, right now.

I am satisfied with the time of my birth and my reasons for being here, and I am not really concerned with the time of what the world will call my death. We, of this teaching, believe that life is eternal, and when the individual has completed this phase of existence, he or she merely passes on to another phase. We believe in the continuity of the individual soul.

OTHER WHYS

Aside from the two basic questions, which seem to have been common to everyone, there have been many other *whys* down through the reaches of time. Early questions were asked to solve simple problems. Way back there, nobody knows when, a man said, "Why can't I get across the river?" Perhaps he learned to swim, but that wasn't always convenient if he was carrying a load. Finally he found a huge log and placed it across the water. Then he could walk across easily. Today we have gigantic bridges, constructed by tremendous engineering skill.

Someone else, in the early days, wanted to move heavy objects without dragging them. He built a crude wheel and invented a cart. A world without wheels would be inconceivable today. Other men wanted to keep track of the passing of time. In ancient days they did this by watching the stars, and that was the beginning of astronomy. Later, men developed the calendar. In this "question-and-answer" manner, ways of meeting needs were found, right down to the present time. Each of the marvelous inventions that have made our current life exceedingly comfortable have been answers to the question *why* and *how*.

All science is based on *why*. There are men and women in laboratories all over the world who are asking themselves, "Why doesn't this work?" Others may be asking, "Why does it work in some particular way, but not in another?" Or, "What do I need to do to make it work?" If they are true thinkers, researchers, and inventors, they all know one thing. They know that if they stick with it, they will get their answer. All scientific work is predicated upon the statement: There is an answer to every question.

Finding the right answer may take a great deal of time. It may take a great deal of work and a great deal of money, but there is always an answer. That is why, in the next hundred years, people will find the answer to what are the cause and cure of cancer and many other things. They may even find the answer to "Why must there be conflict?" Then we may have peace on earth.

Questioning isn't limited to any class of individuals, and it is not limited to adults. When you were about four years old, you went through the most objectionable phase of your growing-up period. At that age every child is in a questioning mood, and each goes through it for about six months. You and I went through it and we were dreadful nuisances. There were the everlasting *whys*. Why does the sun shine? Why does it rain? Why do I have to eat this? Why do I have to go there? Why do I have to wear this? The patience or impatience of the parents made a great deal of sense or nonsense to the child. We'll never know how many of our emotional patterns were formed during that period.

NEVER STOP ASKING QUESTIONS

As adults we still need the word *why*. The moment you arrive at a point where all your questions are answered, you might just as well go on to the next phase of life. You are no longer of value here.

When you pick up a book, a magazine, or a newspaper, don't swallow every statement you read hook, line, and sinker. Take time to think about what you have read, no matter how reputable the author may be. He has put his ideas on paper, and he no doubt believes them. That does not mean that you must always agree. This is important, because any idea that you accept goes into your subconscious memory bank.

I have discovered that much of what we have considered so is not so at all. Here, for instance, is one of my old stories. Because of a generation gap or two, many of you may not even be sure who General John J. Pershing was. My knowledge of this great general of World War I comes from history books, and in them I found a story that always interested me. It was to the effect that when

General Pershing landed in France he went directly to the tomb of General Lafayette, a Frenchman who fought with the colonies in the American Revolution. The story goes that General Pershing stood at attention at the tomb and said: "Lafayette, we are here." There are even drawings depicting this scene. The story was in all of the history books of my generation. It may have been deleted now.

Many years after the war, as Pershing grew older, he knew that the time was at hand when he probably would make his last appearance at an American Legion Convention. At the closing of his speech, he told the Legionnaires that he wanted to make one more denial of that Lafayette story, and he went on record saying there was no truth in it. He said that when he landed in France with those first battalions he went straight to the front, as would be expected. He did not visit Lafayette's tomb until after the war was over.

That's just an unimportant bit of historical information, and believing it or not believing it wouldn't affect your life at all. There are things, however, that you do believe which do affect your life in a negative way. I'm speaking particularly about your prejudices and your set opinions. Why do you have them, and what are you going to do about them?

WEED OUT YOUR PREJUDICES

First of all, what is a prejudice? According to *Webster's New Twentieth Century Dictionary*, a prejudice is "a judgment or opinion formed before the facts are known" or "a judgment or opinion held in disregard of facts that contradict it."

You may be one of the many who dislike a certain group of people. Usually you don't really know why, but your parents and grandparents disliked them, so you do, too. Maybe you don't like the Irish or the English. Perhaps it is the Canadians or the Mexicans. You automatically react with dislike whenever this group is mentioned. If you are an ardent Protestant, you may be annoyed every time you run into a Catholic. If you are an ardent Catholic, you may be annoyed each time you meet someone who adheres to New Thought teaching.

You have these feelings because a pattern was gradually created in your subconscious mind. You weren't actually aware of it, or you didn't give it much thought. This is true of many of the ethnic prejudices in the world today. You profess to dislike, or distrust, those whose racial or political background is different from your own. Ask yourself why. Get to know some of these people as individuals. Some of them will have their prejudices against you and members of your racial or political group. You need not do anything to try to counteract group prejudices. Look to the individuals with whom you have some communication. You will find that they have hopes and aspirations just as you do. They have principles and guidelines that they follow in their search for understanding and achieving a better way of life. You may like what they have to offer.

You probably have heard someone say, "If he's for it, I'm against it." That's a set opinion with no foundation except personal animosity.

Many adults of mature years look at the current trend in hair styles for men and say, "Isn't it awful?" Why is it awful? It may not be progress, because you can look at some old family albums or pictures from earlier centuries and find the same long hair, beards, and moustaches. It is change, however; a new idea for the present generation. Our young men are not standing still and maintaining rigid standards in grooming or sartorial matters. You may not like the effect, but ask yourself, "Is that a reason for condemning them?" Doesn't one of the tenets of our teaching deal expressly with the need for change?

There are socioeconomic prejudices in almost every major city in the United States today. When it comes to housing, which is at a premium in most cities, the rich do not want to let the middle-income citizens into their environment, and the middle-income citizens don't want to be too close to those whom they deem poor.

While we have certain laws regarding job opportunities, there are many prejudices in the field of industry and in the professions. Men and women very often express a dislike for working for a "woman boss." I know of one instance where this was true for a long time, and then the young woman who didn't like having a female supervisor asked herself why. The supervisor was understanding and efficient. Why was she objectionable? The answer involved one of those subconscious mind patterns I've been speaking about.

As a little girl, from the age of two and a half to eight, the young woman employee had been cared for by a maid who disliked her. When a baby brother was born, he got all of the attention and love, while the sister received many severe punishments from the maid. As the girl grew to womanhood, she saw the unpleasant maid in every woman who had any authority over her. That is, she saw the maid until she asked why, and with some help from psychotherapy, found the answer.

There always have been prejudices concerning what is proper work for women and proper work for men. Did you know that in the early days of the telephone industry all telephone operators were men? Then, for a reason which I don't exactly know, women got into the field and for many years women held most, if not all, of the telephone-operator jobs. People have the preconceived idea that there is a feminine "mind set" that is conducive to work in certain fields and not in others. The same can be said, I suppose, of a male "mind set" in higher and better-compensated fields. This undoubtedly will continue to be believed, in spite of the Women's Liberation Movement and equal-rights laws. Are there *whys* that should be asked here?

In our teaching we ordain both men and women as ministers. There have been famous women evangalists and a number of women ministers in the Protestant churches. So far, however, there have never been women priests in the Catholic or Episcopalian churches. I am mentioning this because of a new development that has recently been in the news. The widow of the famous balloonist, Jacques Piccard, is studying to become an Episcopalian priest and hopes that when she has completed the course the ruling against women priests will have been changed.

At the age of seventy-seven, Madame Piccard, who now is a deacon in the Church, confesses that she had wanted to be a priest since she was seven. She became a balloonist three years before her famous husband took up the venture, and declares that free-floating in a balloon gives one a feeling of eternity. Many people undoubtedly will be prejudiced against this woman's desire to live the rest of her days in the priesthood. Again, should they not ask the question *why*?

There is a widespread prejudice against the word spiritual. When it is used people think of something abnormal; something peculiar; something slightly out of this world. They do not relate it to the commonplace things of life. I believe an apple is as spiritual as a gold cross. I believe that everything in essence is spiritual. I believe that every person, in essence, is spiritual. Some people never wake up to that fact.

The world is full of prejudices and set opinions. I doubt if there is any individual who is not beset with a few. Take some time during your busy week and think about your own. You will be amazed when you find how many you have. They are destructive forces. They are like cement blocks in your subconscious mind. You react in accordance with them, and if they were actually cement they would weigh you down.

Suppose you thoroughly dislike someone. This has happened to me several times, because you can't go through life without such experiences. Often I sit back and ask *why*. This person is already off my pathway and on his or her own, but each time I hear the name I react with rigidity, until I finally get the answer to my *why*. I ask the same question when I find that I have a set opinion, some idea which is groundless which I still carry around in my subconscious.

SUPERSTITIONS

Prejudices and set opinions have a close relative that also can delay your mental and spiritual progress. It is superstition. One of the common superstitions is a belief in good or bad luck. It is easy to blame negative experiences on bad luck, and every day of the world people are praying for good luck. They are being misled, because there is no such thing.

I had a person in my office some time ago. She had had nearly fifty years of constant poverty. She had consistently been up against the problems of debt and privation. The story she told was tragic and I tried to show her that her problem was a basic pattern in her subconscious mind. She listened and I thought I had made the point clear. I gave her a spiritual treatment for prosperity and we prepared to say good-bye. As the woman reached the door of my office, she turned and said, "I bought a New York State lottery ticket and I hope it comes in as a result of your prayer." Knowing her basic poverty pattern, I doubt that she won. Perhaps you will say that this was an exceptional experience, but the belief in luck, instead of a steadfast knowing that it takes mental and spiritual work if you want to reach your goal of success, is prevalent throughout the world. Watch your friends and the people you work with. See how often the word luck or its equivalent comes into the conversation.

A couple of years ago I saw a ladder going up to the

second story of a building. I had some time, so I loitered on the corner to see how many people would walk under it. Over a period of from five to eight minutes not a living soul walked under it. They all saw it and walked around it. I looked up to see what the man was doing at the top of the ladder. I didn't want a paint bucket on my head. But there was no paint, so I deliberately walked under the ladder.

We pride ourselves on the scientific world in which we live. We pride ourselves on having overcome a belief in witchcraft and voodoo, yet we hunt for four-leaf clovers and repeat such old sayings as "See a penny, pick it up. All day long you'll have good luck." This is not the way to progress or success. This is not the way to creativity, or to the self-expression for which we were created.

Emerson said that the mind that grows is the uncomfortable mind. This is not an exact quotation, but his meaning is clear. The uncomfortable mind is the one that insists on finding the answers. Ever since I started writing this chapter, a phrase has been running through my mind: *This is the way, walk ye in it.* I've been wondering why these words persisted, and now I know. The way we are to walk is the questioning way, not the way of certainty. Not the way of the person who knows everything, but the way of the person who is seeking the truth and will continue to seek until he finds it.

CHAPTER

X

WHAT
IS TRUTH?

———

Each of us is the invisible individualization of Divine Mind. We are not the past people of psychology, nor are we the extreme past people of theology. We are the today people of Truth.

The third most ancient question that we have had down through the ages is "What is Truth?" The first two, which we already have covered, are "Why was I born?" and "Why must I die?" Man worried about these before he had the intellect to ask "What is Truth?" The question is unanswerable. Jesus didn't answer it. Philosophers have tried to fathom the meaning of Truth and have come up with various concepts, but the question still is being asked throughout the world.

Years ago we had a wonderful teacher on the West Coast, George Edward Burnell, and his classic statement was "The Truth is that which is so." It was that simple. Then he elaborated by saying, "The Truth is that which is so, in contradistinction to that which is not so, but which the five senses tell us is so."

Truth, in our instruction, still is that which is so. It is that which we believe. We believe that the universe is a Unity, a Oneness. It is self-existent. It is spiritual. It is wonderful. Despite what we do with it or what we do to it, it still is a wonderful instrument by which you and I can function and enjoy life. I believe that one of the great reasons for man's existence is for him to be happy.

When I review all the people whom I know who are unhappy I do not sympathize. I am merely concerned because the universe is a place where you and I should have total self-expression, and total self-expression means joy.

A wise man, many years ago, said: "In the world ye have tribulation: but be of good cheer; I have overcome the world." We are individualizations of the same Mind which he individualized, so we are going to overcome the world. We are going to stop believing all the false beliefs we have held up to this time. We are going to believe in the essential goodness of life, the essential goodness of man.

REALITY, ETERNITY AND INFINITY

Philosophers, dealing with what we call Reality, have called it that which is unchanging, that which is all, yet in it, and by means of it, change takes place. Space is not infinity, because space is measured. Time is not eternity because time is measured. Yet there is that which is Infinite and there is that which is Eternal. We are in It, and we always will be in It, because that is the plan of Life Itself.

When you talk to most people about Reality, Eternity, and Infinity, they often seem to be napping. They cannot picture themselves as being more than a ninety-year person. They cannot consider themselves as citizens of an Infinite Process which is forever in action. It is a unity in which separation takes place, but that does not contradict the Unity.

Consider the modern automobile. An automobile is a unity of many working parts, but we do not usually look at a steering wheel, a tire, or the carburetor and say that is all there is. If we do, we are seeing only in part. Most of us, however, look at the whole and say, "What a beautiful car."

In life many people are not seeing the whole. They are seeing in part. They are looking at the steering wheel, a tire, or the carburetor and saying this is all there is. Because they are seeing in part, they are limited to the part they can see. We are always self-conditioned. We are always self-limited. I am. You are. Everyone is. We are limited only by the concepts we have accepted as being true, whether they are true or not. We have accepted them as being true.

I remember my wonderful old aunt who tried to understand what I was talking about, but couldn't. She often would say, "I consider disease perfectly normal. I have to die of something." Personally, I do not believe disease is normal. I don't think I have to die of something. I think I can go to sleep at night and not wake up. That is my plan for the distant future, not for many years to come.

EXPOSE AND EXPAND THE GOOD

It is not the Spirit but the human mind that says disease is normal. It says you have to fight your way through life. The mystics have not said this. The philosophers have not said this. The really great and wise have not said this. Minds such as a Plato, or even as modern as an Emerson, have not said this.

It is the world that has said "Disease is normal." It is the world that has made the other false statements about the roadblocks along man's pathway on this plane of life. If you do not believe as the world believes, you are looked upon as a strange person, a peculiar individual.

There is nothing normal about evil. Only the good is normal. Man has set up every means he can think of to fight evil. It is being handled by all of our sciences. Evil affecting the physical body is taken care of by medicine. Problems of the mind are taken care of by psychotherapy. Problems of world affairs are handled by politics and so on.

We now have to balance this with an equally operative plan for the exposure and expansion of good. This is what we have been doing in the New Thought teaching. Each day we put forth new efforts to expose and expand the good. We leave it to the men and women who believe they know how to do it to get rid of evil. They've been at it since the earliest recorded history and they haven't succeeded yet.

Here and there, however, there has come a Light down through the ages. A person has arisen and said: "Let us put our attention on that which is real. Let us put it on that which is permanent, on that which cannot be measured by the five-sense mind." Such a person put his attention on that which could be intuitively perceived and instinctively realized. He or she knew and believed that good is everywhere evenly present.

Many stories are told of the ending of World War I in 1918. The men who had been at the battlefront, some of them for a year or longer, said that a dreadful peace came over the place where they were when the last shot was fired. They could not understand the silence, although they had known that the end of the war was at hand. They had been used to constant shelling, constant shooting, and constant noise. When all of a sudden it stopped, they were bewildered. They had lost their sensory ability to interpret quiet. It took them time to adjust to the *good*, as I would call it, to that which was *really* so. The good was there all the time, and all it needed was for the guns to stop so it could be exposed, so it could come to attention. The quiet was not something that swooped down all of a sudden. With a lack of evil, the good was exposed. It was there.

In your individual life and mine, I think we spend so much time trying to battle the problems that we don't take time to contemplate the good. Years ago, in an old hymnal which many of you may have used, there was a song: "Count your blessings. Name them one by one." The tune may have been corny but the thought behind the words was in accordance with what I am discussing now: the idea of contemplation of that which is, rather than the continuous sixteen- to eighteen-hour-day fight with that which shouldn't be.

THE LARGER PROCESS

It is no wonder that many of the great world teachers drew apart—went away from the multitudes—not to get away from anyone or anything, but to seek the quiet where they could get their sights so set that they could really see something. They could see that which really was. Then they could go back to their followers and say, "This is the way it is."

Jesus had great difficulty when he tried to gather together his followers. They were all so busy. The fishermen wanted to catch more fish so they could make more money. One man wanted to go back to bury his father. Everyone wanted to do something, except what needed to be done. That was to contemplate great ideas. Finally, Jesus got twelve persons who were willing to at least look at the other side of life. These twelve were individuals who were able to see that there is more to life than tax-collecting, fish-catching, burying the dead, or running a family—all of which they did anyway. They wanted to see the other side of life, because they sensed that it held a great significance.

It is my purpose here to make you aware that you are in a Larger Process than just the business of running your body, your bank account, and your home. There is a Larger Sense to all of life. We go on doing all of the things that are routine in our everyday affairs, but we do them with uplifted vision. We do them with a sense of something greater. That something is the One Mind in which we function, in which we exist, because It created us to exist. We exist in It because there is no way of getting out of It.

We can be thankful that the new thinkers of spiritual concepts have finally removed God from the distance and brought Creative Cause close at hand. They have brought Mind so close that we are a part of It. They have removed the man from the throne in the sky. It has taken nearly a hundred years to do this, but at least for some of us, there is no throne. We know that the Infinite Mind is not a man. We know that It isn't a woman, and we know It isn't an object or a sensation. We know that It is an allness and a completeness. We know that It is a Mind, a Spirit, and a Cause. We know that It must, by Its own nature, create out of Itself. That is what It has done, is doing, and always will be doing. We are in that which is never complete, that which is never finished, that which is forever dying and forever being born.

Some of you will say, "That is all very lovely. But is it practical?" It certainly is. Only the people with a larger vision are valuable to life. The others merely exist. They are ninety-year-program people. What we need to do is to become Eternity programmed, because we always have been, you are now, and you always will be. I always have been, I am now, and I always will be. It is very reassuring to know that.

It is very helpful to have this larger concept, and I am in that which is forever beginning. I am in that which is forever disappearing. All things come to pass, so there is always that which is coming and there is always that which is going. I stand at the center of my soul and perceive it. I am intrigued by it, and it takes away all my fear. I have always been in a field of change, as you have been, and I always will be in the field of change. You always will be.

CHANGE A DIVINE NECESSITY

Change is a Divine necessity. Yet the human mind says "I don't want to change." It does everything it can to prevent change, and seemingly succeeds quite well. In the long run, however, it doesn't. One day Plymouth Rock will be no more, despite what the Daughters of the American Revolution do to keep it. They have it heavily enclosed at the present time, but nature is going to wear it away someday. Nature always wins out.

A million or two years from now, someone may go to Egypt, get on a camel, and find that there are no pyramids left to see. Eventually nature always has its way and things have to change. The necessity of being is change.

Look at the people you know who do not change. They are doing everything they can to prevent change, individually and collectively. Look at them. See their tensions. See their disappointments. See them hanging onto that which they should have released years ago. Watch them clutching things to their bosoms, because they do not want to let go. These are tragic people, even though they do not know it. If they had only released the past, they could have had the greater good which could have followed.

Change opens up the better, the newer, the fresher, the cleaner, and the more inspiring. Many individuals are trying to stand still in consciousness, but actually that is impossible. It is the very nature of consciousness to refuse to let man stand still even though he tries. Everything appears in order to disappear. Ideas come in order to have expression, fulfillment, and then the next larger idea comes along. This goes on throughout all time.

Yet I do not believe that life makes a demand on any person. Life leaves you and me totally free to create or to destroy. I believe that whatever the Power is, whatever the Mind is, whatever the Presence is, it leaves us free. We are not held fast at the end of a string. Infinite Intelligence is not peering at us through a window. It is not trying to keep track of anything. You and I are free agents in a Mind and a Spirit, a Life and a Love that responds but never demands.

LOOK INSIDE YOURSELF

It is true that we live in an age of complexity, and the more complex things become the more urgent it is for you and me to find simpler ways to live. The simple way, which we in the New Thought Movement find effective, is to pause and look inside yourself when the going gets rough. There is an answer in your own mind.

Too many people have not yet discovered this and they keep running around, trying to handle the material problems of their existence in a material way. They are like people riding a merry-go-round. They get on and get off at the same place and nothing has been accomplished. The man at the center, who runs the merry-go-round, has been at the controls. He can stop it anywhere he wants to.

When you are at the center of your own life, when your mind is at the controls, you can determine where you start, and where you stop, and what your real destination is. However, you then will not be running in circles because Life is never circular. It is always spiral. What appears as a circle is nothing but a momentary perception of a movement upward.

The person who goes to the center is in control when he says, "I'm neither name nor number. I am neither child nor parent. I am neither husband nor wife. At the center I am not nationality. I am the creative power, and I determine what I shall see, hear, taste, touch, and smell. I am the determining factor at the center of my own soul and my own life."

You stand at a center of control over your experience when you stop being human and start being what you know you are. The time has come to put off humanity and to assume Divinity, because you always have been Divine. You and I and everyone else always has been a part of the Divine Mind which created us. Many people, however, do not know this, so they act like frail humans instead of like spiritual beings.

Jesus tried to tell the people that they were Divine. He said it in many ways. He said: "Ye are the light of the world." At another time he asked, "Is it not written in your law, I said, Ye are gods?" He also told the disciples that anything he could do, they could do, and they could even do greater things.

What is your interior perspective of yourself? Sooner or later Life makes us find ourselves. You ask: "What am I? Who am I, and what is this whole thing about?" When you arrive at those questions, you have arrived at the threshold of the Spirit. These are questions that no theology can answer. You have to answer them yourself.

There is a center of clear knowing within you. The Bible calls it "Christ in you, the hope of glory." It is a point of knowing where, in your aloneness but not loneliness, you discard name and number and see yourself as the expectation of the ages.

YOUR REAL ESTATE

This, of course, is a play on words. I am not referring to any piece of property you may own, but to your real place in the scheme of life. Concepts which we stress in our teaching are correct self-understanding and correct self-appreciation. There have been so many years of believing that it was not spiritually correct to like ourselves. This was pounded into us by our parents, our grandparents, and by the very culture in which we functioned. The tradition that man is unworthy has come down through the ages.

The concept of human unworthiness has been common to almost all religions, and we can't blame Christianity for it. In fact, it is much older than the Bible. Ancient cultures, Egyptian, Chinese, and others, believed that *man is not worthy* and *man is prone to error.*

Our teaching, about one hundred years old, started with the proposition that if Jesus, who said he was one with the Creative Power, could do great things, then this was an inheritance for all of us. We started with the concept that *man is worthy of everything that his own mind can conceive.* That is why we have a statement on our printed matter: "What mind can conceive, man can achieve."

This is what we believe, yet we find the old patterns still lurking at the backdoors of our minds. Occasionally we hear someone in our teaching say, "I guess it wasn't meant to be." This is a fallacy. What happens in your experience is a matter of mental assumption. What mind can conceive, man can achieve. When I use the word conceive here, I mean a depth acceptance, not an "I would like to have" or "I would like to be." Rather you say: "This I am going to have" and "This I shall be."

That is what I call a depth acceptance. It is an assumption, a conception that is not merely a conscious mind attitude. It has gone down below into the subconscious mind. It has gone into that great arena of consciousness which does the work when given direction. It has moved into depth acceptance and the wheels start turning. You do not, with the conscious mind, have to figure out how an event, a situation, or a condition is going to take place. This is not your business. It is your business to know Truth, and the Truth sets you free into whatever it is you want.

Every once in a while there comes a glimmer in your own mind. There comes a sense of possibility, a moment of Truth wherein you are able to conceive for yourself. You are able to take a pure idea out of your mind and say to yourself: "This I shall have. This I shall be." You do not do this because the people in your neighborhood do it. You conceive your idea for yourself, not for someone else, even though what you conceive may later bless and benefit many people. This idea is your *real estate*. The only thing you actually own is your conscious and your subconscious mind. This is your only property.

THAT WHICH IS REALLY GOOD

What do you believe is really good? I believe that Life is good. Love is good. Order, harmony, beauty, and joy are good. Either I have them or I don't. But I can have all the good there is if I want it, because it is a free gift. I do not earn it. I merely have to awaken to it. I merely have to perceive it and mentally accept it. This universe still has in it so much that is good and it is waiting for those who have eyes to see and ears to hear.

It is very interesting that one day Jesus said to people with perfect sight and perfect hearing, "Blessed are your eyes, for they see; and your ears, for they hear." He was telling them about the "Larger Picture." This larger concept is also to be found in Eastern teachings. They present the belief that, at the very point where negation is, there is the good to be perceived by anyone who can perceive it. He who can perceive it can do so because he knows it is there. He who doesn't know it can never see it, because he believes his five senses entirely.

I use my five senses. I let the world report to me everything it needs to report through my five senses, but I keep a larger vision. I know that I am not merely body and I am not merely intellect. I try not to be caught up in limitations. When we are caught, we do not see that which is. We do not hear that which is. We do not taste, touch, or smell that which is really so. Our whole attention is fixed on "How can I fight this next battle in my individual life? I have this to overcome. I have that to overcome."

Your attention is a powerful instrument. Move it to the mountaintop and you will find that the valley becomes beautiful. It is not without reason that the mystics have used mountains as illustrations. On the opening page of my book *The Power of Decision** I use the famous poem, "Give Me Men to Match My Mountains," meaning the people who can see more than a three-dimensional world in trouble, this mountaintop sense of being that is the Truth.

It isn't the whole truth because no one can ever know the whole truth—that which I really am and that which you really are. But you can say quietly in your own thought: *I am in and I am a part of that which is beyond Infinity and Eternity; that which is forever creating out of itself; that which is forever providing the new, which I may have if I will let go of the old; forever offering me the different if I only will let go of the monotonous.*

The Bible says, "Behold I make all things new, sayeth the Lord." It doesn't say, "I am going to keep everything around as long as I can."

Let us rejoice that there have been people who have let this newness come through. Let us be thankful for the pioneers who started this teaching. They premised their instruction on a new idea: that life is not preparation for a heaven you go to after death. It is an experience right here and right now. Some people were dismayed, but many heard the new idea gladly, because their own reasoning had made them realize that the old idea wasn't so. They accepted the Larger Concept. This is not a final one, because everything always has been a revelation followed

* This poem appears in the first edition only.

by another revelation. This is the way it is, because Mind never repeats Itself. Life never repeats Itself. Love never repeats Itself.

Always something makes the new. We have had the fresh wind go through many theological halls, clear out the dust, clear out the old forms, beautiful perhaps in their day. They are not for us in this day.

We know that there is one Infinite Eternal Cause. We know that we are operating in It. We know that we have It to use as Mind. We know that the subconscious mind acts as a law of creation. We know that the world is in trouble, but the way to end it is not to increase the trouble. So we are looking to the mountaintops and keeping our vision high. We are doing what needs to be done at the logical level to offset the problems of the world, but that is not where our vision stops. We are people who are walking tall, seeing something that is there to be seen when it is sought.

Good is everywhere evenly present, but you have to look for it or you will never see it. Seek your own invisibility and you will find God.

IMMEASURABLE MIND

IMMEASURABLE MIND

Let us do what we do in our classes once in a while: close our eyes and relax. Our hands are relaxed. We are relaxed except where our clothes touch the body. We are aware of that, and also of our feet touching the floor.

Do you realize that you extend into infinity?

You may or may not be able to feel the skin on your forehead. I can't feel my ears, but I know they are there—although I cannot sense where they leave off and space begins. The same with my nose and chin.

This makes me realize that *I* am the one who defines myself as body, whereas in metaphysics we define ourselves as idea. Or, taking another term, we say we are consciousness. Here we have a free-flowing term that is as old as the ancients and as modern as now. It says that you and I are an activity of thought and feeling, moving through a continuum of Mind.

Today's talk is not intended to be practical. But remember, anything that is practical is always preceded by an expansion of consciousness in the individual, because groups expand only as individuals expand.

An address delivered by Dr. Barker to the Alumni Association Meeting of the First Church of Religious Science, New York City, May 1967.

When we begin to think, "I am consciousness," for us *consciousness* is an individual term. I am sure when you first heard it, it had no meaning whatsoever. It was an abstract concept. But having read, studied, and attended classes, your saying "I am consciousness" opens up the trapdoor to infinity. Something begins to work in the mind that is not conditioned by dimensionality—a free-flowing thing, yet never out of balance, never getting into psychism, and never peculiar the way the world would call it peculiar.

All of this has to do with your having a larger concept of yourself, because the immeasurable you, the invisible you, is you as you stand in infinity and eternity. It is all about *that* concept of you—not just *any* concept of yourself, or some concept *by you*, but rather a concept of an Infinite Being, an Infinite Mind, an Infinite Knower. It includes the past, the present, and the future—that which sees you as a citizen of infinity and unity.

We catch this only in our high moments. It is a thing that can rarely be caught, and you will lose it in materialism. The materialists cannot grasp it; therefore they have their saints and saviours, hells and heaven. They have to have a location. They have to have a geography of life after death.

But we have emerged from that. Something has led us —not a person, but a yearning in our own thought, an inclination to the right teacher, to the right education, to the right consideration—and the thing that has led us is not a god. Rather, it is the God that we are. And it has not led us as much as it has *impelled* us, because it had to come from the center.

It has not come through a psychic revelation. It has come not in a word, but as a soundless perception. It has come as intuition, but as the intuition that is clear, that is pure knowing, rather than as the intuition that can still be interpreted by us.

Let's say that you have a hunch to buy something; that is intuition. There is still an element of choice in it; you could still go to a shop, look around, and not buy. But the clear knowing that expands consciousness is intuitive knowing that is beyond question or beyond saying "no" to. This is when you and I move out a bit—where definitions have less meaning, where lines of distinction are less meaningful. In the past this has been called the mystical experience—a term I would rather not use. It has been incorrectly used too often.

At the center of me is the hidden purpose of an Infinite Something which by means of me—it can't be any other way—is temporarily incomplete in expression. We who are working in consciousness are opening the trapdoors of the mind so that more of this Something can come through. It is not guidance—it is knowingness. It is not leading us anywhere; it is not taking us anywhere. It is merely opening us up to a larger sense of what we are. Here we move from the practical to the straight absolute or pure knowing.

This intuitive sense deals not with getting, with going somewhere; and it has little to do with becoming. No, the trapdoors are opening for your larger *self-appraisal*—not to make you richer or happier. They are opening to let you know, if you want to know, your real self (an over-used term); what you are, have been, and will be.

Traditional Christianity has done so much damage with its assumption that we did not arrive from anywhere and are going to heaven or hell. We have thrown that out the window, raising the question: if these theological concepts are not so, then what *is* so?

The result is that a great many people, even within Christianity, reject life after death totally. I can't agree with them, but I can respect their belief. Or people move to the fascinating study of psychism in order to understand the next plane; or to reincarnation to understand the process of rebirth. All of which are theories, which I cannot disclaim nor do I have to accept. About reincarnation, I still don't know; and I have read some of the better material on it.

However, I do know this: I am an unfolding consciousness; and when you become vitally interested in being an unfolding consciousness and let the trapdoors of pure knowing open, there comes a point when you don't care what the method is on the physical level. You say, "If I come back, that is okay; if not, that is okay too. But I, as I, go on forever, even if nameless and numberless."

People will say, "Doctor Barker, that is only because you and people like you want the human ego to survive." That is right. I no longer separate the human ego from the Divine Ego, any more than I separate the human mind from the Divine Mind, or the process of origination from the totality of Absolute Being.

Nor do I denounce personality, because the Infinite *is* person *as me*. Therefore if I have a human ego, I did not create it, and, if I did not create it, then it is a divine ego —an ego necessary for individuality to express Itself through knowing Itself.

The doctrine of selfishness has possibly reasserted itself in the New Thought movement as a doctrine of selflessness and brotherhood, which we would perhaps be better off without, because, as you know, the world has been enriched by individuals rather than by collectivism. We are teaching a divine selfishness in a divine selflessness. The ego is individuality maintaining and expanding Itself. We would say, in our language, that it is God *in* man *as* man, knowing Itself as God, but not as man.

The very word *man* indicates a lesser status. When we say "God and man," we have the big and the little, the total and the partial. I am trying to get rid of that. I am trying to get rid of it by realizing, *through direct knowing*, that instead of seeing myself as the lesser, I open myself up to see myself perhaps not yet as the total, but as expanding toward it.

In pure reasoning along this absolute line, the word *man* should be changed to *individuality*—for there is only that, forever individualizing Itself for self-expression. Individuality is the explanation of the totality that is individualizing Itself as individuality.

Remember, I said that this would not be a practical talk, except that you will feel better when it is over—and not because it is over. It is too easy to say you are greater than you think, because there you can fall in the trapdoor of wrong use of ego. But in pure knowing you can't, because in pure knowing you are expanding your present opinion of yourself—so that the opinion is as nothing.

I come back to the question, What am I in infinity and eternity?—or, as Maurice Nicoll would say, What am I that is beyond time and space?

What I am is more than time and space, because these are measurements. I am dealing with that which cannot be measured. Space is as much of infinity as we can be aware of, and time is only that much of eternity as we can measure now. Instead, I am dealing with that which has not yet been measured and timed.

In this thing, what am I? I am consciousness. Does this mean I am not matter? Of course not—because matter is consciousness, because form is consciousness. There is nothing in the absolute concept of yourself that negates form.

True, there is that which sees form as density, form as weight, form as limitation, and form as just "Oh, Lord, do I *have* to get up and get dressed, eat, take the subway and go to work?" However, I am not dealing with that. I am dealing with outline, color, and substance, rather than with density and weight, which automatically include limitation.

Nor am I dealing with what man will be or individuality will be. I do not even know what I shall be next week, so how can I know what I shall be a billion years from now? Yet that which I am not, I know that I can be next week.

I let consciousness flow along because it will frighten me to break its flow by worrying about some distant future. The Infinite already has that well in charge; and what the Infinite does, It does in the atmosphere of love, which is the very opposite of fear.

I was about to refer to our "individual self-consciousness"—but I wonder if it *is* self-consciousness, since, again, this would suggest separation between the Infinite and individuality. I see you and myself as the individuality individualizing the totality, with the trapdoors of the mind open for these concepts that come as *knowing*—not as leading or guiding—so that I know myself from a larger viewpoint. But not for the purpose of gain. For that, I would go back to the textbook* and subconscious mind, to law and treatment.

It is probably just as well that our real being is beyond imagination. If we could ever know what the Infinite knows us as being, we would probably try to top the other person. And yet this disclosure would seem as unlikely for us as the golden streets of heaven are impossible to us now.

One of my early teachers said that if I healed only one person, then my ministry would have fulfilled itself on earth. Of course, she and I both knew that I would heal more than one person, and I am sure I have done it. But her point was that if you help even only one person by consciousness, and not on any other level, you have evidenced your spiritual knowing.

Now, you and I can help each other, but we can't know each other. It is the old adage that you can bring a horse to water but you can't make it drink. Knowing is that intimate, personal thing. It is like your "I am"—which is what it really is. We are dealing with the most intimate aspect of consciousness.

I can share ideas, but I cannot share that which is beyond ideas; and what I am talking about is beyond ideas. It is even beyond your concept of yourself—and yet it is not psychism. I do not believe a normal God does things in an abnormal way. I believe in psychic phenomena, but I'm not sure they have anything to do with God (rather than simply with the abilities of certain people).

* *The Science of Mind*, by Ernest Holmes.

The knowingness that I am talking about is not really communicable; it is only self-digested. It may be communicable in the sense that others see you expand and do not even know what it is they are seeing. That, in the long run, is the only communication there is—beyond the communication of ideas. It is a communication so subtle that the five senses are baffled by it, if they even sense it, because here again you are dealing with total individuality—so total that, while it shares with others, it does not need them.

To me, this explains why Jesus could die and not weep over his family. He had arrived at the consciousness that metaphysicians feel he must have arrived at. He had arrived at the awareness that *includes* others but does not *need* others. Anything that it gives to others is a free gift, because there is nothing that the other can lend to it. It is pure consciousness, knowing Itself, offering Itself to others, but still independent of others.

That is you in time and space. Does it mean you do not have loved ones? I assume that it means you *do* have loved ones, because you always have to give. You need it far more than receiving.

Every time I get in a tight spot in regard to money and I write out checks to charities, money begins to flow in. When my money tightens up, it indicates a need to give. Pure consciousness says, "Doctor Barker, you have blocked the channels; open them up."

It is natural for consciousness to give, and it has nothing to do with receiving. That is why the old nonsense of "giving it to God" is ridiculous. Ernest Holmes says that the Divine Infinite is a divine givingness. He doesn't say that It is receiving; he says that It is an infinite *givingness*.

The Infinite knows that which you and I are trying to know—that because we are individualizations of divine givingness, there is no depletion possible. The intellect objects to this and says, "Wait a minute!" But in divine knowingness, we are not impeded by intellect.

Are you and I to conclude that we shall be completely transformed by all this? Of course not. Maybe in twenty billion years we shall be. But at least we can move toward the goal. Some of you become weary of the eternal use of Science of Mind to have health, wealth, love, and self-expression. In my capacity as teacher, I get even wearier of it. But it is such an improvement on the old thought!

The talk that I am giving couldn't be given to our weekly radio audience. Every radio would have been turned off by now, because the man and the woman of today are so utterly fascinated by today, with no interpretation of it in terms of tomorrow, except for a will, insurance, and a plot of ground. The average person in your office or neighborhood is concerned about tomorrow only in terms of financial security in the last years and a will, which will cause family arguments.

Today's person is tremendously interested in today and should be. I am, too—but not with the usual stuff we have served up to us. I am also vitally interested in tomorrow; but I want a larger concept, even if it is true that I can come back by means of a medium to you people. And may I add: if you ever do get a message, it is not me—because I am not coming back that way. Even if I could, I wouldn't want to.

No, I want a concept of something more than whether there are houses and gardens where I am going. I am not living just to go somewhere. I am living to go *everywhere*; so I will go where there are houses and gardens and chat with Mrs. Eddy and Ernest Holmes and a few others. *But I want to go on and on*, and I want to go on as *expanded consciousness.*

However, the more I define the next plane, the longer I shall be there. The more I define myself here in nothing but materiality, the longer it will take me to wake up out of materiality. But, beloved, you and I are not what we are seeing at the moment, nor what we are listening to at the moment. We are the Immeasurable Mind.

MEDITATION / TREATMENT

There is One Infinite Pure Being. This being is what we are—nameless, numberless, timeless, spaceless. We are pure being in absolute consciousness. The trapdoors of the mind let in the expanded concepts so that when we say, "I am that I am," the first *I am* will not be name, height, weight, and bankbook. It will be pure consciousness. The second *I am* will not be form; it will be pure being. We are pure consciousness. We are that absolute total pure consciousness. We leave the details of the procession through infinity and eternity to the Wisdom that gave us the right body here, the right things for our comfort and care. If that is what the Totality of Being did here, It will do it everywhere. We are now the citizens of the everywhere.

So be it!